"What could happen if you do nothing?"

A Manager's Handbook for Coaching Conversations

JANE MURPHY

WITH KHATUN HUBER

Published by Giraffe Business Publishing LLC
April 2010

Giraffe Business Publishing LLC
708 Third Avenue
New York, NY 10017
www.giraffebusinesspublishing.com

Giraffe Business Publishing LLC is a registered trademark

Copyright © 2010 Jane Murphy
All rights reserved.

ISBN 10: 0-9844262-0-5
ISBN 13: 978-0-9844262-0-1

Printed in the United States of America

Library of Congress Control Number: 2010901119
"What could happen if you do nothing?":
A manager's handbook for coaching conversations /Jane Murphy with Khatun Huber
ISBN 978-0-9844262-0-1

Cover and interior illustrations copyright © Jerry Murphy
All rights reserved.

Book design by Don Charles Design

Contents

What to suggest 129

4. Conversation Maps

Situation 1: Managing up

Situation 2: A change effort in response to financial setbacks

Situation 3: Defining and maintaining recruitment standards

Situation 4: Helping clarify and improve gaps in performance

This Book

Coaching is about positive, lasting change. Increasingly, businesses are recognizing the value it brings to the workplace. Coaching isn't "touchy-feely" stuff, although it's based on trust and respect—words often found in corporate values statements!

The coach is a guide in a collaborative process that uses listening and questioning to move an individual or group of individuals forward—in their thinking and in their performance. It's a humanistic way to deliver real rewards to those being coached and to the business.

Managers don't have all the answers, nor should they expect to. But they should expect to make the most of their people in order to develop and leverage the capabilities of those they manage.

"What could happen if you do nothing?" is an easy-access resource to help you add coaching skills to your management repertoire or expand the coaching skills you already have. The focus is on how to listen and how to question in order to help employees deepen their thinking and take action to meet challenges and maximize their own potential. It's powerful stuff that, for a manager, goes to the heart of being a leader.

Manager	"You really shifted into high gear just now. I hear conviction behind what you're saying."
Rachel	"You do? I guess this matters more to me than I thought."

Active listening can shine a light, offering new insight to the person doing the talking.

Dave	"Could you repeat that?"
Manager	"I asked you, 'What could happen if you do nothing?'"
Dave	"Hmmm, I hadn't considered that. I suppose if I did nothing, he might take some initiative, which is exactly what he needs to do on this project."

The *right question in the right context* can trigger new thinking and more successful interactions.

Manager	"Have you ever considered hitting the pause button when that happens?"
Lori	"I do tend to jump right in. Wouldn't hurt to take a wait-and-see position."

Suggesting a different tactic here offers an alternative to a knee-jerk, emotionally charged response. It can set the stage for healthier interactions and faster resolutions. However, a coach is not there to provide answers or do the "coachee's" work. The coach's role is to steer the process, to lead her coachee to discovery and changed behavior. That said, making a suggestion can sometimes prove fruitful, especially if the coach's repeated attempts have failed to elicit from the coachee new thinking, a reframed point of view, or proactive initiatives.

This book's what, why, how, and when?

What

Communication is one of the biggest challenges in corporate life and critical to moving forward, for individual employees and for the business. Indeed, change begins with a conversation. Every conversation introduces an occasion to coach—to open the door for another person to recognize an opportunity to enhance performance, to discover strengths he already has, to generate solutions to a challenge.

This handbook uses mini-dialogues to demonstrate the impact of engaged listening, deliberative questioning, and animating suggestions in facilitating change.

Your capacity to integrate coaching into your management repertoire will prove a significant measure of your leadership capability, particularly in conversations regarding performance challenges. You will see this for yourself time and again as you help guide your people to draw upon their own smarts to explore and discover the answers they already have. It's critical to recruit and develop your people as a way to meet business goals. Simply put, you are the supervisor of your people's performance and the steward of their development.

Why

"Coach" is one of the many hats that effective managers wear to drive a culture of positive change and accountability in the workplace. In their coaching capacity, managers engage in a potent mix of listening, asking, and occasional suggesting. At its core, coaching is a conversation—in fact, many conversations—that helps someone take measurable steps toward a clear goal. The process facilitates an individual's effort to change and enables that individual to deliver on it.

Coaching conversations are based on trust and confidentiality, enabling the coachee to feel safe, heard, and supported—an important foundation for effective change. Your role as a manager should not conflict with your ability to ensure trust and confidentiality when coaching your people. If you ever tackle a topic that must be shared with others, then you need to clearly explain this with your coachee.

Hopefully, you will find this handbook useful when you are considering how to stretch someone's thinking, energize him, harness his potential, and motivate him to achieve a higher level of performance. This "someone" is likely to be an individual whom you supervise, maybe a high-potential, or GenYer who has learned to expect ongoing feedback and a more collaborative management style. But it could be a peer, a more senior employee, or even your boss.

So what, precisely, could be the benefits of coaching?

For the business: across-the-board performance improvement	For you and your coachee: a toolkit of skills and behaviors for professional growth
▼ Higher productivity and performance for all levels of employees and managers	▼ More effective leadership
▼ Improved job engagement and retention	▼ Strengthened communication with direct reports, peers, and upper management
▼ Better alignment of individual performance with business goals	▼ Increased self-awareness
▼ Stronger teams	▼ Expanded, deeper thinking
▼ Enhanced leadership development	▼ Healthy and productive work relationshipis

How

"What could happen if…" is a "flip to the page you need" resource. Nothing complicated to navigate. Listening, asking, and suggesting are the three main parts of what's between these covers. And these building blocks of the coaching conversation are integrated—listening gener-

ates questions, which in turn invite further active listening; appropriate suggestions occur organically as the conversation evolves.

Coaching conversations are spirals that go around as they move a dialogue ahead. They zig and zag and don't follow a clean line from beginning to end. Coaching is an iterative and animated process whose script gets written in real time. And these conversations don't necessarily end with a solution. In fact, as a colleague has shared, some of her most powerful coaching sessions end "openly." The coachee takes away thoughts to sit with and consider. Then he returns with greater awareness and new thinking.

A caveat: Culture and personality are critical factors in developing a dialogue. Just as people differ in their learning styles, they also differ in how they communicate. Certain cultures are more hierarchical, and people tend to look up to the boss. Other cultures are more collegial and participatory. Some individuals are assertive communicators, others more collaborative. Tuning in to style and cultural differences should inform the way you listen and frame your questions and comments.

When

An infinite variety of challenges can trigger business- and work-related conversations. Whatever issue your coachee is trying to tackle, you can use this handbook to boost your coaching capability. Chapter 2, "Asking" addresses typical dilemmas and challenges.

Keep in mind that any conversation can become a coaching conversation. Opportunities can present themselves

- ▾ At prearranged meetings
- ▾ One-on-one or with your team
- ▾ As a series of sessions

Coaching conversations can be useful in many business situations—during a change initiative, a critical vendor negotiation, a merger or acquisition, a customer-satisfaction analysis, a performance review.

Sometimes you may find yourself going round and round in a conversation and want to encourage your coachee to consider new options, put aside business as usual, think more intensely. Asking "What could you do about this?" or "Who would you like to be in this situation?" can interrupt the coachee's "stuckness" in the drama of a circumstance and help move her thinking along. Turn to "Know when to interrupt" (p. 35). You may have heard contradictory comments and consider that maybe discussing values could help clarify intentions. Check out the "Values" questions (p. 76).

Perhaps your report has set an ambitious goal and promised delivery in short order. You're dubious, but you don't want to deflate his enthusiasm or display a lack of confidence in his ability. Browse through the "Reality" questions (p.56) to consider how you could help him think through his commitment and his plan of action in the context of SMART (specific, measurable, achievable, relevant, time-based) goals.

Read through the "Listening Guidelines" (p. 16) to be sure you are picking up on the cues she may be offering. For example, her lack of enthusiasm about the marketing data could reflect her concern that it's not legitimate. Or the fact that he mentions his training in negotiation techniques could suggest opportunities for a more important role in sales strategy.

Or maybe you've been meeting with one of your managers who seems apathetic and unengaged. He acknowledges that recent cutbacks have resulted in added stress and a much heavier workload. He feels he's caught on a treadmill of simply eating, sleeping, and working. Listen very carefully for what he may not be saying. Has he mentioned feeling isolated or unacknowledged? If that's the case, you might pursue a line of questioning that would tap these feelings and suggest positive steps he could take to explore professional outreach, such as joining a professional association. Perhaps you haven't expressed your appreciation of his struggle to cope with fewer resources.

Whatever the circumstance—performance review, professional development, or team building—try to keep in mind the essential coaching behaviors, your guide to moving through the conversation in a way that is useful and fruitful.

Essential coaching behaviors

▼ **Presence:** Be in the moment. Get rid of any internal or external distractions.

▼ **Coherence:** Be clear and succinct in your questions and comments.

▼ **Placement:** Establish where you both are in the conversation.

▼ **Framing (and reframing):** Provide a perspective or context.

▼ **Clarification:** Distill what's been said and play back the salient information.

▼ **Paraphrasing:** Summarize or restate what you've heard.

▼ **Feedback:** Focus on performance, not on the person.

▼ **Acknowledgment and respect:** Recognize, empathize, understand— these are important measures in validating someone's worth, feelings, and contributions.

The mission of this book is to help you develop a coaching orientation in your management style, particularly in the way you communicate. Improving how well you listen, question, and suggest—developing a style that "pulls" rather than "pushes"—will become second nature. Learning to manage in a way that unlocks insight is like learning to play the piano. Initially you wrestle with translating the notes on the page. Eventually, your fingers just read them and make them sing.

| "What could happen if you do nothing?"

1. Listening

What's it like when someone listens to you intently for more than five minutes? Imagine you're at a dinner party, sitting next to the host's uncle, who hardly touches his crème brulée as you regale him with your whitewater rafting exploits. Likely you'll walk away with a great impression of him but without realizing quite why.

"OK, that's true, but I'm a manager, not a dinner party guest. I'm up to my ears in projects with deadlines. Why should I be concerned about listening when I have to keep the ball rolling?"

"Because active listening pays rich dividends."

"What is active listening, exactly?"

When you listen intently to someone, silently focusing on what the person has to say, you're likely to learn something of value. It's different from "hearing," which is merely being aware of the words but not necessarily their content.

Taking the time to listen in a focused way is critical to effective management. Research shows that active listening can save time and money as well as ensure better alignment between individual performance and business goals. Industry studies have documented impressive return on investment for companies that have made a commitment to coaching. For example, a Fortune 500 telecom study by MetrixGlobal found that executive coaching produced a 529 percent ROI. Met Life, in measuring the success of one particular corporate coaching program, found a 35 percent increase in productivity among sales force participants.

Listening is as important a part of conversation as talking…maybe more so. **Go beyond the words being said. Go for the whole message.**

Sharpened listening fosters

- ▾ A more complete understanding of a situation

- ▾ Valuable insight into another person's thinking, which can produce consequential solutions

- ▾ A demonstration of your interest and concern for other perspectives and experiences

- ▾ Acknowledgment and validation of your people

- ▾ Stronger rapport

- ▾ More cohesive teams

Listening is work. It takes discipline not to superimpose our views, finish people's sentences for them, add our two cents, or let our mind wander. If you can master a concentrated approach to listening, the floodgates will open, and facts, thoughts, beliefs, emotions, needs, hopes, and expectations will flow. This valuable information will help you manage successfully.

When you listen intently without interrupting, you are giving the other person room to talk and think. A profound result of affording him this space is that it gives him the opportunity to hear himself and assess what he is saying and thinking.

Listen up!

According to the International Listening Association, the top three distractions that prevent business professionals from listening well are

▼ Environmental
(phones, people talking)

▼ Personal or internal
(hunger, headache, other preoccupation)

▼ A tendency to rebut or develop a counterclaim while the speaker is still speaking

Have you had the discouraging experience of trying to talk to someone as he is answering the phone, glancing at the computer screen, or gazing out the window? It's like being tuned out.

How about being on the phone with someone and suddenly, mid-conversation, sensing the discomfort of dead air? You just know he's checking his email!

Multitasking: NOT

Talking on a mobile phone while driving isn't multitasking. Neither is talking on the phone while reviewing a marketing report. Research shows that we don't multitask...our brains are actually switching from one activity to the other. In fact, it's estimated that interruptions such as so-called multitasking cost the U.S. economy nearly $650 billion annually.

Jonathan B. Spira, chief analyst, Basex

Don't go there yourself. Important nuggets of information crucial to your work, the business, and your people can be lost when you fail to pay attention to the speaker. Not only is your behavior demeaning to the person who's talking, but you've also squashed any potential learning to be harnessed from the conversation in which you're "supposed to be" participating.

We may think that technology enables us to multitask, but actually our brains have not yet caught up. We can really "do" only one thing at a time. It's also true that we think faster than we talk. That's one reason your mind may tend to wander while you're listening.

Quiet the outside and the inside.

- ▾ Get rid of external distractions so you can really pay attention to the person in front of you. Put aside the report you're working on.

- ▾ Clear yourself of internal sources of distraction like thoughts about personal issues, the day's news, or the tuna sandwich you're planning on having for lunch.

Remember, **people have different styles of communication,** often expressed in the way they speak. So if you're a fast talker and they like to take their time, ditch your impatience and allow them to think. It's a great opportunity to gather facts, separate the content from the feelings, and get a handle on another point of view—information that will guide you both to better decisions.

When you're in coaching mode, you must leave your biases behind. It's essential that coaching be nonjudgmental. Remember, **there are no "right" answers, only useful answers.**

You may be driving these conversations, managing the process, but the person you're coaching is in charge of the content. It's critical you remain open to her thinking and what she has to say. Bring your curiosity to the table. There are lots of things to listen for.

Hear ye, hear ye...
Listening Guidelines

- ▼ Listen for potential.
- ▼ Listen for what's not said.
- ▼ Listen for inconsistency.
- ▼ Identify nonverbal signals.
- ▼ Listen for perspective.
- ▼ Listen for energy.
- ▼ Listen for themes and threads.
- ▼ Listen for what's behind the words.
- ▼ Listen through the silence.
- ▼ Listen for positive change.
- ▼ Acknowledge you're listening.
- ▼ Know when to interrupt.

LISTEN FOR POTENTIAL

Manager "What resources do you need to make this project really fly?"

Greg "Thanks for asking. I was going to talk to you about that. We could really use an extra laptop for Alex since he's been doing some traveling to the new account. And we could also use the conference room a couple of mornings a week so we have a bigger space for brainstorming. People would be much more comfortable than being squeezed into my office."

Manager "I'll see what I can do. So you're confident everyone can meet the deadlines?"

Greg "Absolutely...the team is fantastic. In fact, everyone knows they can always come to me with their ideas and concerns. I enjoy the back and forth and being there for guidance. So, can you really get us the laptop and the conference room?"

As you "listen" to this dialogue, ask yourself if you're hearing any clues for potential—that "something special": might Greg's concern and suggestions about his team reflect a talent for mentoring? **Between the lines, little gems may signal hidden capabilities, impressive emotional intelligence, or a wealth of potential that isn't being tapped.** Even a funny streak is an aptitude to be mined and put to effective use.

Hidden capabilities may arise in other contexts:

▼ Does she refer to a previous job whose skill set she could utilize in her current role?

▼ Does his "go to" attitude and ready encouragement toward the people involved in a project tell you he's a natural team leader?

▼ Does she mention competencies that might be better leveraged if she assumed a different role on the team?

▼ Does her command or knowledge of a particular area indicate a promotion might be in order?

▼ Do his strengths suggest a great pairing with another colleague or department?

Listen for What's Not Said

In the following dialogue, Jonah works for a company that has recently reorganized...Jonah is now leading a new team. His manager is following up with everyone who's been impacted by the changes. He particularly wants to talk with Jonah, who is a team player but can be uncomfortable with conflict and hesitate to speak up when things aren't going well.

Manager	"I was hoping we could touch base today and see how things are going for you and your new team."
Jonah	"Oh right, the new team. It's pretty much what I expected, really. We beat our milestones this quarter, etc., etc."
Manager	"I know! That's great! But you don't sound so thrilled about it. Is there something I'm missing?"
Jonah	"Things are OK."
Manager	"What could make them better?"
Jonah	"Honestly, I miss the give and take of the old group.Everyone here just sort of puts their head down and does their own thing. The work gets done, but the fun is gone. My old team was always looking past the next milestone and debating where we wanted to be to deliver the product ahead of the deadline...and where we'd have our party!"
Manager	"Teams can take awhile to really come together. What would it take for that to happen sooner with your new crew?"

Talk *can* be cheap. *Or* it can be rich. **Often, what's *not* said is more telling than what is.** Jonah's manager picks up on his disappointment and leads Jonah to share valuable insights that he can leverage to impact his team's engagement and performance.

Sharpen those antennae to pick up on anything that is being glossed over or avoided. Emotion is a factor. Seemingly neutral words may be delivered with positive or negative feeling. What's underneath? Satisfaction? Resentment? Boredom? A sense of accomplishment? Frustration? Enthusiasm? More interesting, is bad news delivered in undisguised tones of happiness—or vice versa? Hmmm.

It would be easy to hustle Jonah out of the room as soon as you hear the words "beat our milestones"! But he sounds bored, doesn't he? Or is it resentment you're hearing? Fatigue? It's worth looking into to find out what it is exactly and, more important, what can be done about it.

Manager	"You spoke about wanting more regular meetings with me. Are there particular things you want to discuss?"
Jamie	"Um...well...Yeah, I guess. Maybe the project we're working on this month? Or...a few things, maybe...really...I'm not..."
Manager	"Yes?"
Jamie	"Sorry...I'm not...It's fine, actually."
Manager	"OK, but it sounds like there's something on your mind. How can I help you?"

Delivery can be telling. Does she hesitate at certain places? Does she avoid the central issue or wander off into irrelevant facts or events? Do the rhythms of her speech and the words she chooses suggest a searching for something more palatable than truthful? Is there obvious nervousness around particular subjects? Is there confidence and assuredness about others?

Manager	"How much time do you think you'll need to train our new marketing manager?"
Bart	"I hadn't really thought about it. I mean, I have to get the IT guys in this week for something else, which is really annoying because they're always busy. And of course, I have no assistant next week. Oh, and I've been planning the company picnic this year, and I'm not sure yet where we should have it... So, what do you think? The park or the beach?"
Manager	"Wherever it is, I'm sure we'll all look forward to it. But about the marketing manager: you're the point person on that, and we have a lot riding on when she is fully up to speed. We have the Maple Foods people coming in two weeks from now, and the new person will need to know what she's talking about. So we need to set a deadline."
Bart	"We do...?"
Manager	"I'm hearing how busy you are right now. Is there anything you could put off or delegate?"

Where is Bart headed? Does he get into extraordinary detail on a project and lose the forest for the trees, seemingly out of touch with impacts on cost and time? Does he get sidetracked or bogged down in details? Does he need to be reined in, or is there simply too much on his plate?

Manager　　"How did the meeting go with the clients?"

Lucy　　"You know the project manager they just brought in? He took up so much oxygen with all his questions. And then there was something wrong with the projector, so we only got through half of his PowerPoint. I left without sign-off from Murray, who was out sick. So, no financial OK will delay us another few days, at least."

Is the glass half empty? Some people have a tendency to harp on the things that *aren't* going right. Do they ever focus on solutions, ideas, answers? Or is the half-empty glass really a character issue? Here is an opportunity to ask her about what *is* working, what's "right." (See Chapter 2, "Asking.")

Is she able to connect the dots and spot the relationships between things? Is there a sense of cause and effect, or an ability and openness to adjust tactics along the way?

Figure out figure-ground

Two optical illusions:

The Rubin Vase, set against a black background, can be seen as either a vase or two faces.

Likewise, the Canadian flag can be "read" as a maple leaf...or...two arguing faces.

*"There's so much to do and lots of moving parts.
I hope we meet our milestones and our deadline."*

This guy *is* on target but expressing uncertainty. Is what he's saying inconsistent with the way things really are? He might be somewhat skeptical, but the milestone graph behind him reflects on time, on target performance.

"Watch" what's said

In communications relating to feelings and attitudes

- ▼ 7 percent is in the words that are spoken
- ▼ 38 percent is in the way the words are said
- ▼ 55 percent is in facial expression

Professor Albert Mehrabian, UCLA

Active listening could reveal inconsistencies in his perceptions and the real status of his work and performance.

It can also inform a line of questioning that can resolve what appears to be conflicting information. If he's on target so far, does he see trouble ahead? Or is this a matter of needing better feedback and acknowledgment?

Check your own nonverbal signals! Does your posture express openness, do you maintain eye contact, and do you nod to encourage the speaker? Next, attend to the nonverbal signals he is sending. These physical behaviors can signal high or low interest, insecurity or self-assurance, distraction, discomfort, lack of clarity, high engagement, or avoidance. Watch for these nonverbal cues, and use this information in your questioning. Address with curiosity what you observe.

As a manager, you may think having the kids at the office
for Bring the Kids to Work Day is a great idea...
Others may not.

We each have a point of view. It's like different camera angles portraying the same scene—high, low, side, over the shoulder, or wide angle views portray different perspectives. Likewise, our perspective (our take on reality) depends on where we are situated! This point of view might be based on our experience, expertise, responsibilities, prejudices, assumptions, cultural background, the "functional culture" of the particular department in which we work (marketing, production, etc.), or simply the information available to us.

You can detect a person's perspective by considering factors like these:

- ▼ How does her culture help define her?

- ▼ What is his orientation toward time (deadlines), position (organizational hierarchy), and expectations (responsibility)?

- ▼ What are her intentions?

- ▼ What values has he expressed?

- ▼ What needs is she communicating?

- ▼ Who are the stakeholders in his performance?

And even...

- ▼ What is his perception of *you*?

Left brain or right brain? Detail or big picture? Top down or bottom up?

He's more likely to respond to numbers on a graph than to someone describing the plan.

She's extremely collaborative but has difficulty with command-and-control types.

She's a task-oriented micromanager, definitely not good at delegating.

He loves brainstorming. Watch out, though—he can get so wrapped up in generating new ideas, he loses track of time and deadlines.

So, put yourself in their shoes. How might things look from their perspective? And how might YOU look? (It's a great learning opportunity to see yourself as others see you!)

Consider how a person's unique perspective may create blind spots or signal the need for a broader view. How informed is his expressed opinion, given his situation or position?

- ▾ Is he missing critical information?

- ▾ Do his views align with the values and goals of the business?

- ▾ Is he so insulated that he doesn't understand the impact of his actions on other stakeholders?

- ▾ Is he so deep in the weeds that he's lost a grip on the whole project?

And while you're at it, ask yourself:

- ▾ How informed am I, given my situation or position?

- ▾ Am I missing critical information?

- ▾ Do my views align with the values and goals of the person I am speaking with?

- ▾ Am I also insulated in any way?

- ▾ Do I need to have a better understanding of the situation?

Manager "Thanks for coming in. I wanted to kick around some ideas with you about where we can take the Johnson account."

Madeline "Oh. Don't you don't think it's going well?"

Manager "No, no. On the contrary, I think—"

Madeline "But you see problems with it? You know the team has worked really hard for months."

Manager "Yes, I know. I simply wanted to check in and share some ideas with you. Now I'm a little confused. Why do you think there are problems? Are there problems?"

The manager in this situation is caught off guard. He isn't expecting Madeline's defensiveness. Now he's wondering if, in fact, things aren't going well with the Johnson account. Here's an opportunity for him to use his coaching skills to tease out what's behind Madeline's seeming concern. He will learn, through open-ended questioning and acknowledgment of his respect for Madeline's opinions, that everything truly *is* fine. The fear of being judged by him is what underlies her defensiveness. Such a revelation offers this manager an opportunity to become more sensitive to his people's reactions to his assessments of performance and how he delivers that feedback. This is bound to translate into better communication and a healthier working relationship.

Different people can hear the same thing very differently.

It can be astonishing to learn that you perceive a conversation, and the intentions behind it, in quite a different way than someone else does. People can hear the same thing very differently, even to the point of taking away contrary messages. This can result in confusion, loss of valuable time, hurt feelings, and even a general breakdown in communication. It's important for both parties to understand what each actually *means* by the words they use because each can interpret identical words differently.

The energy behind the words often influences how the message is interpreted. Wide eyes and animated gestures indicate high energy. But what sort of high energy? Anger? Enthusiasm? Panic? How can you tell? Similarly, low energy might be read in a bored stare or hands flopped at the sides. Is this boredom? Or fatigue? Perhaps disappointment?

Bear in mind that each of us expresses our own energy level differently. So, one person's calm demeanor may be another's ambivalence. Getting to really know your people will allow you to distinguish one attitude from the other. Meanwhile, here are some things to listen and look for:

▼ Are his gestures accompanied by a smile? Or a frown?

▼ Is she speaking in a monotone?

▼ Does the volume of his voice change at the mention of certain subjects or themes? If so, which ones, and how?

▼ Does she emphasize certain words but not others?

▼ Does he seem distracted? If so, when?

People's energy can change as they move through a conversation. It's worth picking up on these changes across the landscape of the conversation. Notice where, when, and how.

Vinny is a people person, a water cooler kind of guy. His manager sees a lot of potential there, but he's been concerned that Vinny is not as engaged with the work as he is with his co-workers. They've had two conversations, which his manager introduced as an informal review. The manager drew upon his coaching skills to enable Vinny to think about how he spends his time and what he values about his position as a junior product developer.

These talks have revealed Vinny's need for opportunities to collaborate. They agree he could coordinate with marketing and sales to produce an integrated report on the upcoming rollout for Estelle, the new senior VP, when she arrives next week. The manager suggests Vinny put everything together on one page of the company intranet. Vinny is happy to work with people from the other departments. The manager has tapped some energy reserve. The two agree to meet again, just before the SVP's visit.

Manager "You've done a great job on this report. It definitely presents the big picture. I'm sure Estelle will be wowed. How do you feel about it?"

Vinny "Yeah, I think it captures the status of the rollout, numbers-wise and brand-wise. Doing it gave me a chance to sit around the table with Lauren and Doug. I have a better understanding of what sales and marketing are up against with budget and schedule issues. Product people grumble a lot about marketing and sales, but I don't think it's all that justified."

Manager "Any suggestions on what could be done to work better with them?"

Vinny "Working with them more upstream would be helpful. More regular meetings. Wouldn't hurt for some of them to sit in on our brainstorming sessions too—when we have them!"

Listen for Themes, Threads, and Patterns

Whether in one conversation or over the course of many, threads and themes can emerge. You may notice someone coming up against the same roadblocks over and over again, or demonstrating an ability to readily adapt or change tactics. There may be clues to behavior—positive or negative. For example, in conversations with your coachee, particular interests may keep surfacing that could help define a course for further development.

Here are a few things to consider:

▾ How does she give praise where praise is due?

▾ Does she complain a lot, either generally or about the same thing?

▾ How is he at collaborating?

▾ Is he in constant turf wars with other departments or co-workers?

▾ Does she always blame others or make excuses when faced with responsibility for something going wrong?

▾ Is she highly self-aware, self-critical? How does she demonstrate this?

▾ Does she constantly worry about things that are low on the priority list?

▾ Is he good at delegating?

▾ Does he express interest or good ideas about things outside the purview of his job?

▾ Is she experiencing a frequent lack of acknowledgment for her achievements? How do you know this?

Listen for What's Behind the Words

Lara has been meeting with her manager to try to work through her frustration with her team. She had felt that managing their project was like herding cats and that they spent a lot of time going over the same territory. The conversations with her manager have revealed a need for better project management. For her part, Lara has acknowledged her strengths as a team player: stronger on motivation than on planning. In between her initial grumbling and her clear desire to improve team performance, she mentioned almost as an aside that she functions better within clearly defined schedules but doesn't like managing them. Her manager picks up on Lara's discovery about her own strengths and the gaps in the team's strengths. His questioning helps Lara identify the need for a strong project manager to step in and work with the team. Lara suggests bringing Nigel in from another department to help harness the team and develop a milestone plan. This subsequent conversation reflects the early benefits of the coaching and the resulting changes.

Lara	"I thought the meeting went really well. The agenda was clear, everyone was on the same page, and we were able to walk through the status report and move on to our next milestones pretty quickly."
Manager	"Sounds like you're comfortable with Nigel's lead on the project...and his celebrated 'attention to detail.' How are things for you now that he's on board?"
Lara	"He really took the pressure off, and I feel much more confident that I can keep everyone focused on the work and not on interpersonal agendas about who's doing what. Everyone is clear on goals and expectations."

A particular untapped area of expertise or a particular skill set, a preference for a highly organized style of working, a desire to be more involved upstream in brainstorming and co-creating—these are all examples of the hidden messages that can be embedded in a conversation.

Occasionally, we read between the lines. This "listening to what's behind the words" requires close attention to things that the speaker has said but hasn't necessarily identified as important. Calling out this "buried" intelligence, or subtext, can more quickly move the person to action with a clear focus.

Consider other subtexts:

▾ Are feelings, hopes, fears, or hesitancy coming through?

▾ Is she signaling her individual ethics or values? Are they being compromised or supported?

▾ Is she expressing confusion and a need for clarification?

▾ Does she consistently articulate where her project fits into the overall strategy? Could she be a candidate to represent the plan to the board?

LISTEN THROUGH THE SILENCE

Silence is said to be golden; it can also be eloquent. However, in everyday life few of us feel comfortable with too long a silence in the presence of others. This tolerance can even vary by culture; discomfort may set in after a few seconds or not until nearly a minute has passed.

We're all familiar with the experience of standing in a crowded elevator: how excruciatingly conscious we are of the silence and how awkward it can feel. Even with the closest of friends or family, gaps in conversation can be quite a challenge to endure. This is a shame because silence can be very informative. If you can learn to "sit with" the silence, it can

Silence speaks

"As eloquent as he was...what was more eloquent was the silence of two million people listening."

Nancy Pelosi, commenting on President Obama's inauguration

- ▼ Allow the speaker time to think…to gather and form his thoughts into words

- ▼ Provide you with time to think as well

- ▼ Give the speaker permission to slow down her thought processes and come up with useful observations and ideas, instead of feeling she must jump in with something—anything—to fill the gap

- ▼ Point up a trigger to the silences, which may be worth exploring

Take note:

- ▼ Where do the silences occur?

- ▼ Does she seem uncomfortable and lost for words? Or is she just mulling the situation over?

- ▼ Is he nervous in your presence when you're silent?

- ▼ Does the silence create room for good ideas?

LISTEN FOR POSITIVE CHANGE

Remember Lara, who brought Nigel in to help structure the project schedule her team was confused about? Angela, normally a chronic complainer, is on Lara's team. Lara's manager has been in touch with all the team members since Nigel stepped in to work with them.

Angela "Do you have a few minutes to hear about yesterday's team meeting?"

Manager "Of course, but I thought we were going to discuss it tomorrow."

Angela "I know, but I couldn't wait to tell you!"

Manager "You sound buzzed about it; it must have gone well this time around."

Angela "Yes. Everyone was prepared, on time, and ready to go. And we were all on the same page. Even Margaret and Arthur. They actually agreed to collaborate on the market survey design!"

Too often, we focus on the negative. In fact, complaining and finding fault can become a habit. Although awareness of a problem is essential, it's the ability to measure and acknowledge positive change that will really move things forward.

Measure progress against the content of previous conversations or job performance. You can also read his verbal cues and body language to detect improvement—even when the person does not directly toot his own horn.

Beyond your own particular performance criteria, what else might indicate progress?

- ▾ Has her tone of voice changed to reflect enthusiasm or a better outlook?

- ▾ Does he complain less? Smile more?

- ▾ Does his body language reveal more confidence?

- ▾ Is she keen to fill you in on what her team has achieved?

- ▾ Does he now see things from a broader perspective?

Acknowledge that You're Listening

Jeff	"I'm really not quite sure where I am with this issue or where to start..."
Manager	"OK. Tell me."
Jeff	"So I'm worried about the new receptionist. She's really not doing her job properly, and it puts me in a bit of a dilemma."
Manager	"How so?"
Jeff	"Because I'm the one that pushed for her to be brought in."
Manager	"Uh-huh...."
Jeff	"Although...I did have an idea..."
Manager	"Hmmm..."
Jeff	"Well, I think I'll ask Regina to have a chat with her about expectations here. Regina originally started as the receptionist. Seems like eons ago, but she was terrific...Yes, I think I'll give that a try and see if Regina can help turn her around."

We all love to be listened to. Not only that, but during any conversation we appreciate little reminders that someone is interested. Nods, *uh-huhs*, and smiles are validating and encouraging. They let the person know you're interested and engaged in what she has to say and encourage her to go further with her thinking. Verbal acknowledgment is also crucial on the telephone.

As mentioned earlier, we can all hear the "dead air" that occurs when someone is *not* listening! Commonly, these subtle acknowledgments of listening are enough to help someone stay on track with a line of thought without your having to do much at all (except to listen!).

Know When to Interrupt

Occasionally we find ourselves losing the thread of a conversation. Or the coachee can get so involved in the drama of the situation that he doesn't see a way to move on. Your instinct may be to politely let him carry on, hoping you'll eventually "catch up" and make sense of what he's saying or that, in the grip of the drama, he'll suddenly gain another perspective. But this often doesn't happen, so we tune out because we think of interrupting as something "bad" or "rude."

However, in a coaching conversation, **strategic interrupting can be very clarifying and productive for both parties.** How and when it is done is key to unruffled feathers!

Bob:

"But that was before the merger,... or was it after? Anyway, he was very concerned about whatever it was and so was everyone else. And either then, or later, like I said..."

Bob's Manager:

"Could I ask you to clarify that last piece for me? I'm not clear on who said what and when, and also how it links to what we're discussing."

Interrupt when

- ▾ You feel that you or the other person has lost the thread.

- ▾ You need clarification to fully get what's going on.

- ▾ It might be helpful to reframe or offer another way to look at a situation to help the coachee "come unstuck" from the drama.

- ▾ The coachee needs to refocus.

- ▾ Some placement is called for—that is, stating where both of you are in the conversation…the story so far. It's also an effective way to keep the conversation on course and on topic!

- ▾ There's an opportunity to offer a suggestion. Perhaps, with the person's permission, you can offer something useful to consider (see Chapter 3, "Suggesting").

Listening: What's the big idea?

High-powered listening is truly a matter of being "all ears" (and eyes). It takes practice and discipline. Again, it is often a matter of going beyond the words, picking up on what's *not* said, what's underneath what *is* said, and *how* it is said. All these ways of listening combine to derive the fullest meaning from what is being communicated. Active listening will offer you, the manager/coach, breakthroughs in your coaching and valuable information to use in developing your people and enhancing business performance.

2. Asking

Successful coaching conversations are a bit like jazz. There's improvisation and reciprocity. The process is more organic than strategic. Responses to questions generate new questions, which trigger different responses, which suggest entirely different lines of questioning (see Chapter 4, "Conversation Maps," p. 135). However, it's important to keep in mind that whatever questions you ask, you should frame them to

- ▾ Expand thinking

- ▾ Encourage consideration of other points of view

- ▾ Reveal hidden strengths and potential

- ▾ Open options for action

There are several lists of sample questions in this handbook to help you build an inventory that you can internalize and draw upon in preparing for a coaching opportunity or follow-up session. They are *not* meant to be memorized. And

An interesting notion... don't you think?

"No man really becomes a fool until he stops asking questions."

Charles P. Steinmetz, the engineer who developed alternating current

you shouldn't refer to them during a coaching conversation. Questions organically arise from your listening. Coach in the moment. Don't try to summon up your next question *while* you're listening. Use your gut instinct, your intuition, to formulate your questions.

"What should I ask?" you ask. Managers who motivate, like teachers who inspire, understand that asking open-ended questions, rather than those orchestrated to produce the "right answer," get the imagination and insight flowing. They encourage people to come up with their own ideas. In business, that can pay big dividends—both in engagement and in revenue.

"What actionable items are left on your deliverables list?"

"You mean, what do I have left to do?"

Business shorthand or heavy use of jargon can be anathema to some and totally OK for others. Consider the person you're talking to. Be sensitive about the words you choose and how you frame a question. Remember also that a person's culture, bias, mood, and learning and communication styles can influence how she receives and understands your questions and therefore how successful those questions will be in generating new and deeper thinking.

Coaching isn't therapy. Coaching conversations are meant to drive things forward. There's no rear-view mirror. The emphasis should be on today and tomorrow, *not* yesterday, even when a discussion is focused on remediation.

Stick to "how" and "what" questions. These tend to expand thinking, reveal hidden strengths, and promote forward momentum, which creates options for action.

"Why" questions can send us backward into unproductive blaming. Consider the contrast here: "WHAT would it take for you to deliver your next report on time?" vs. "WHY didn't you get this report in on time?" You'll be much more effective when you ask someone to focus forward on what he can add to improve matters or how she might do things differently!

Make sure you leave adequate time for your questions to be answered (listening again!). Don't stack questions one on top of another. It's likely, as you wait and watch, that you will be able to hear (and see) her thinking. Then, when you have your answer, you may still need some clarification. If you haven't understood, ask!

While you're listening...listen. Avoid trying to come up with your next question. If what you're hearing doesn't suggest a particular question but you want to encourage your coachee to dig deeper in his thinking, consider basic questions that gently encourage more thoughtful consideration:

▾ Why is that?

▾ Tell me more...

▾ So what does that say to you?

▾ Has your thinking changed about this? How?

▾ What could you do? What are your choices here?

▾ How do you feel about this? What would make you feel different?

▾ What's the opportunity here?

Beyond a cache of simple questions like these, which promote expanded thinking, there are endless approaches to building a larger inventory of questions.

In this handbook, lines of questioning are organized into three sections:

- ▼ Process: questions that serve the three key stages of a conversation

- ▼ Tactics: strategies that deepen thinking and encourage action

- ▼ Topics and Themes: questions segmented according to topics that commonly arise in business, and themes that influence behavior and the change process itself (such as time management, engagement, etc.).

This arrangement isn't meant to suggest that the question groupings are discrete. Every conversation follows its own beginning, middle and end (the process) and usually tackles a particular challenge (the topic or theme). You will guide the process by using some of the tactics of open-ended questioning.

Each section introduces a number of focus areas for discussion. Many (particularly in the "Topics and Themes" section) suggest infinite lists of questions and variations on the same question. This is to demonstrate the range of questioning available to encourage deeper thinking. The question lists offered here are a start and will hopefully encourage you to expand on them yourself.

The Process

Every conversation has a beginning, a middle, and an end.

You can draw upon your coaching skills in any conversation—even those that occur at the last minute or unexpectedly. Be opportunistic and coach in the moment as it presents itself. However, when you are helping someone tackle a challenge, you are likely to have more than one conversation on the topic. In formal coaching, each conversation is considered a "session," and the sum of all conversations is "the engagement." There is an arc, or sequence, in both a session and an engagement. In your coaching conversations as a manager, the arc will reflect your guidance in helping your coachee define his objective (his desired change), identify actions to take to reach that objective, and successfully engage in making that change.

Like a story, a conversation has no set path for moving ahead. Some stories use flashbacks or jump back and forth in time. Again, conversations—especially coaching conversations—don't follow a straight line. However, like a story, **every coaching conversation should have a beginning, a middle, and an end.** There are questions that serve to open the conversation (beginning), to clarify or reframe the conversation by placing things midway (middle), and to take stock and look ahead to close the conversation (end).

OPENING

After an initial informal, relaxed exchange, there's the business of getting down to business. Be sure to **set the time frame for the conversation and ensure the confidentiality of the discussion and your desire to facilitate the change** that has been or will be identified. The kick-off to a conversation focused on a challenge or dilemma suggests a host of opening questions. Subsequent (follow-up) conversations on the topic open differently, acknowledging and building on the previous dialogues.

Getting started

- ▾ What's up?

- ▾ What ground do you want to cover today?

- ▾ When you say you're not sure about the project, which part of it would you like to discuss with me?

- ▾ How would it feel to devote a series of meetings to making this a reality?

- ▾ How do you feel about dedicating the time to make this happen?

- ▾ How much is "a lot of time"?

- ▾ Where do you want to be after you've worked through this challenge?

Let 'er rip!

"The secret to getting ahead is getting started."

Mark Twain

- ▾ What do you want to achieve here?

- ▾ What's your vision of the perfect outcome?

- ▾ What would you like to walk away with or get some clarity on today?

- ▾ We have about a half hour for this; where would you like to get to in that time?

- ▾ If we call reaching your goal 100 percent, where are you now?

- ▾ By when do you want this to be the case?

- ▾ If that seems a bit ambitious now, can you suggest some beginning steps you can take to start you on your way?

- ▾ From where you are now, what would be the first step that you could feel OK about? What's the next step?

- ▾ How much of this situation do you feel is within your control?

- ▾ How much are you willing to invest in this process?

_____

_____

_____

Follow-up starters

- ▾ What happened since we last spoke?

- ▾ What have you learned?

- ▾ What could you do differently?

- ▾ How have your actions changed your goal?

- ▾ What did you do well? What did you discover as a result?

- ▾ What were the highlights of this project? What did you learn?

- ▾ What is working?

- ▾ What's not working? What can be done about that?

- ▾ What's a next step here?

- ▾ When do you think you'll get there?

- ▾ What else do you need? Who could help in this?

- ▾ When should we touch base on this again?

_____

_____

_____

Be sure you're on the same page and have the same understanding of what's on the table.

At different junctures in a coaching conversation (certainly by midway) it's important to pause and assess where you are, to paraphrase what's been said and interpret it, based on your understanding. **Take time to offer a "this is what I hear you saying" recap of what you've understood.** The coachee can then verify or correct this "playback." Playback can even trigger insight, since the coachee is hearing an interpretation of her own words. Her message is objectified when she hears it coming back at her from someone else. If your take-away matches the intent of the message, then this placement, this "taking stock," serves as a validation for your coachee.

Clarifying inconsistencies

- ▼ Here's what I see. Here's what I hear you saying.

- ▼ Here's what we know so far.

- ▼ So let's see if I'm on track with you…

- ▼ Let's see where we are…

- ▼ How about we step back for a moment and look at a few different ideas…

- ▼ So you want to fire so-and-so but with minimal pain for everyone?

- ▼ Did I hear you correctly when you said…?

- ▼ Am I missing something here?

Building on what's been said and moving the conversation ahead

- ▼ What impact is thinking about this having on you?

- ▼ What are you noticing about your thinking? What insights are you having?

- ▼ How could you deepen this understanding or go further with it?

- ▼ Do you know what to do to turn this into a habit?

- ▼ Are you clear about what to do next?

- ▼ Do you know what to do next and just need a sounding board, or are you really stuck?

- ▼ What options do you have for changing things?

- ▼ How can I best help you with your thinking on this?

- ▼ Do you want to think this issue through with me right now?

- ▼ How much time would you like to spend on this?

- ▼ May I reframe it for you?

- ▼ What would be the benefits of doing that? What would you lose?

- ▼ How might you ensure that the same problems will not arise again?

- ▼ What would you have to change? What could you do to make that happen? Who could you ask to change other parts?

- ▼ If you were able to change all those parts, how well would your needs be met?

_____

_____

_____

Closing and Closure

A conversation may have a natural endpoint, but most coaching conversations need to be managed within the time allotted. You need to prepare the other person when the clock is nearing the time to end. Be sure to leave enough time to summarize, look ahead to next steps and milestones in advance of your next conversation, and reach out for feedback on your own participation in the dialogue.

Manager   "You've come a long way over the past six months and seem to be moving ahead. Would you like to continue with a monthly chat about this?"

Carlos   "Good question. Actually, I feel like I'm good to go. I think I can handle it from here—although these meetings have been really helpful, so it'd be great to check in now and again."

Manager   "Absolutely. How about either of us reaches out if something comes up or if we want to brainstorm anything?"

Carlos   "That would be great, thanks."

Closing refers to winding up one conversation *or* concluding a series of conversations. Closure refers to completion or the meeting of an established goal. The next sets of questions apply to closing one discussion and to closure after a series of conversations. When a series of discussions reaches its natural conclusion over a period of weeks or months, you will both be looking at what you have achieved overall: the measurable results and the change effort in general. After this, ongoing maintenance or a checking-in plan can prove beneficial.

Winding down and looking ahead

Closing a single conversation:

- ▾ We have a few minutes left; shall we review some next steps?

- ▾ What would you like to do next?

- ▾ Who needs to know what your plans are?

- ▾ What support do you need? From whom?

- ▾ What have you learned?

- ▾ Where do you want to be with this when we meet next week?

- ▾ On a scale of one to ten, how certain are you that you will accomplish this by your milestone date?

- ▾ How can you make that closer to a ten?

_____

_____

_____

Closure after a series of conversations:

- ▾ Do you feel you've met your goal against the benchmarks you set when we started?

- ▾ How confident are you about fully taking the reins at this point?

- ▾ Would it be helpful to review what you've achieved here?

- ▾ Would you like to have an occasional check-in, as needed?

- ▾ How will you incorporate this learning into your general approach with your staff?

_____

_____

_____

Feedback

Feedback to you, as manager and guide in the conversation(s), is useful both at the end of each meeting and at the endpoint of a whole series.

Closing after a single conversation:

- ▾ Did we miss anything?

- ▾ How can I support you?

- ▾ What worked? What didn't? Was there something I missed?

- ▾ What can I do differently next time to help you in this effort?

Closure after a series of conversations:

- ▾ Going forward, is there anything you anticipate wanting to check in about?

- ▾ What have you learned from this experience?

- ▾ What was your most valuable take-away? How will you use it?

- ▾ Is there anything in the way I've approached this challenge with you that you think I could improve upon next time?

- ▾ What was unexpected about this process?

The Tactics

Tactics are the steps you choose to reach a desired outcome. As a manager who is coaching one of your people through a change, you can follow a variety of tactics in your questioning. The more comfortable you become in assuming a coaching role, and the more you engage in these forward-oriented conversations, the more likely you will be able to internalize effective tactical courses to pursue.

Manager   "OK, I understand. You're saying your team feels the workload is more like overload. Is that how *you* see it? ...What's been said in the team that backs up your perception? ...Does anyone see it differently?"

Managers who are skillful in guiding coaching conversations use questions that leverage these tactics:

- ▼ Stretch and encourage elaboration

- ▼ Deepen thinking and encourage discovery

- ▼ Energize

- ▼ Clarify

- ▼ Trigger action

- ▼ Sustain change

This is not to suggest that you plan your questions ahead of time. Remember the importance of being in the moment—of being "present"— and coming to the conversation in an unbiased way. It's more a matter of **strategically guiding a conversation in real time, in response to the information you are receiving** and how you are being presented with that information. So, if you've learned about a perceived excess of work, get him to dig deeper and explore whether it's true or not and what can be done about it. By reflecting back his answer, you've let him know you've understood. Then follow up with something designed to get him thinking more about it. Don't cluster the questions before he has a chance to answer, but build your questions on his answers.

This tactic of layering, of building questions, is like one by one opening those Russian nesting dolls, revealing the littlest doll in the center. Metaphorically, this smallest doll hidden inside all the layers is the nugget, the kernel that you're working to reveal which will hopefully point the way to a solution. These questioning tactics get people's brains engaged!

Again, powerful questions can encourage new thinking, deeper thinking. Focusing on a person's thought process itself can shine a light on where he tends to stop considering new options or how she can move the lens to focus on new details, new perspectives.

▼ How do you usually think about things? What's your style? Are you a big-picture thinker, or do you begin with the details? Do you think more with your head or your heart?

> **Brain trust**
>
> "How do I know what I think until I hear what I say?"
>
> *Tallulah Bankhead*

▼ Do you focus more on the way things are or the way they could be?

▼ Is there a place where you do your best thinking?

▼ What insights are you having?

▼ How could you go further with it?

▼ What needs to change in order for you to get where you want to be? How long have you been thinking about this? How frequently?

▼ How important is it to think about this?

▼ What impact is thinking about this issue having on you?

▼ What do you know? What do you not know?

▼ How can I best help you with your thinking on this?

▼ Do you WANT to think about this?

▼ Spending more time thinking about this might make you feel…how?

- ▼ What's your gut reading of this situation?

- ▼ How clear is your thinking on this? How could it get clearer?

- ▼ Would you like to brainstorm this idea? Tell me more about it? What else?

- ▼ How much time would you like to spend on this?

- ▼ How important is this issue for you, on a scale of one to ten?

- ▼ What could you do differently?

- ▼ How clear are you about what to do next? Do you know what you need in order to move forward with this?

- ▼ When you say you're not sure about the project, which part of it would you like to talk over?

Ground Them in Reality

Questions can wake a person up to the facts as they are, not as he wishes them to be or as he might misconstrue them. Focusing on stakeholders introduces a more holistic view of how the coachee's actions impact others or how other people's perspectives might impact his understanding.

- ▼ Who else is affected by this?

- ▼ Who knows about your wanting to do something about it?

- ▾ How much control do you personally have over the outcome?

- ▾ Who else has some control? How much?

Which end is up?

"Are you really sure that a floor can't also be a ceiling?"

M. C. Escher

- ▾ Who are the other stakeholders in the outcome?

- ▾ What action steps have you taken so far?

- ▾ Are you feeling any satisfaction from this?

- ▾ What, if any, resistance do you have to acting on this?

- ▾ What resources do you already have (skill, time, enthusiasm, money, support)?

- ▾ What else will you need? Where could you get this?

- ▾ How do these circumstances compare to where you were with this last year?

- ▾ On a scale of one to ten, how certain are you that you will be able to accomplish this by the deadline you set? What can you do to move the likelihood closer to ten?

- ▾ What alternatives have you considered?

- ▾ What are the risks that you see here? How can you manage them?

- ▾ Is doing this absolutely necessary? What might be an alternative?

_____

_____

_____

Ian   "Every time someone suggests something, she raises an objection. She doesn't get it...her idea of brainstorming is to play with everyone's brains. I try to acknowledge her point of view, but then of course I have to get the team back on track and focused on solutions. It's easy to criticize. Much harder to come up with answers."

Manager   "What could happen if you didn't do anything?"

Ian   "You mean just let her carry on punching holes in everyone's ideas?"

Manager   "Yeah. Sorta. What could happen?"

Ian   "Hmmm. I guess she'd eventually run out of steam, or someone else might tell her where to put it. Maybe I don't give her enough time to even hear herself or let the others turn things around and encourage her ideas. I'm always primed to referee when she's around."

Exploring "what ifs" offers the opportunity to consider different actions and how they might result in different outcomes. Many of us often operate based on what we consider "givens." So having a manager/coach encourage thinking about other options can upset the applecart (in a good way!) and reframe the problem. These questions can free someone who's boxed in by assumptions:

- ▼ If you didn't do that, what could happen?

- ▼ If you did that, what could happen?

- ▼ What's the worst that could happen?

- ▼ What if you felt less stressed? More energetic?

- ▼ What's the best that could happen?

- ▼ What if you waited for him to come to you?

- ▼ What if you initiated the conversation?

- ▾ What if you invited them to your next meeting?

- ▾ What if you met somewhere else, outside the office? How could that change things?

- ▾ What if you didn't hire her?

- ▾ What if you didn't fire him?

- ▾ What if you did work from home two days a week?

_____

_____

_____

Look at Options

Encouraging, even prodding, the coachee to consider a variety of choices can open the door to opportunities that were there all along, but hidden. It can take some digging to get at certain ideas.

More is better

"The best way to have a good idea is to have a lot of ideas."

Linus Pauling

- ▾ What are some options you could pursue, going forward?

- ▾ What would be a really big step?

- ▾ What's a first step?

- ▾ What else could you do? And what else...?

- ▾ What if you could have the "ideal" situation...what would that look like?

- ▾ What would you do if you had more time? A larger budget? If you were the boss?

▼ What would you do if you could start again with a clean slate? A new team?

▼ What's risky here?

▼ What are the pros? The cons?

▼ Which of these solutions appeals to you most?

▼ Which would give you the most satisfaction? How so?

▼ What's worked before?

▼ Which part of this is most holding you back?

▼ How do you feel about the way you're tackling this project overall (chaotic, organized, disciplined)?

▼ Can you look at this from her perspective? What do you see? What could this suggest?

▼ How do you feel when you think about putting this off?

▼ What would make this decision easier?

_____

_____

_____

"For a change, first let's look at what we HAVE accomplished. Then we can talk about what still needs to get done."

Figure-ground refers to the cognitive ability to separate visual elements based upon contrast...dark and light, subject and background, trees (details) and forest (big picture). When the viewer changes focus, a whole different picture emerges. You can use this principle, with a little poetic license, in coaching conversations.

Let's assume that the coachee has been focusing on one aspect of or perspective on a situation, but hasn't considered a different point of view... the background or context in which it occurs. Suggesting that the coachee stand in someone else's shoes and consider a different take on a given situation can generate new insight. So can a change of perspective: in dealing with frustration over a team's reduced productivity, helping the coachee refocus on what might seem an inconsequential factor—such as the lack of a needed resource—could prove quite consequential in helping her reach a workable solution.

- ▼ I understand your frustration with the new demands coming from the sales team. What new demands do you think they are facing?

- ▼ That has had a big impact on you. Could you characterize its impact on me?

- ▼ You've been understandably focused on your presentation. Where does it fit with the agenda for the whole conference?

- ▼ The team has been pretty clear with you about their concerns. Have you shared your concerns with them?

- ▼ What's another perspective you could take on this?

- ▼ You've obviously been consumed by this. When are you not thinking about it? How does that feel?

- ▼ So, what *didn't* you say? What didn't *he* say?

- ▼ OK, you've talked a bit about what's not working. What *is* working?

- ▼ I hear a lot of dissatisfaction with her performance. When *has* she performed well? How have you known?

- ▼ When *is* he actually engaged? How can you tell?

- ▼ You've been in immediate-response mode over this. What if you don't do anything?

CLARIFY WHAT'S BEEN SAID

Manager   "So let me see if I understand you correctly. You believe if you could staff up by one and outsource some of the design work—since we're already so overloaded here—your group could handle this new account? And you've budgeted for these changes?"

Bruce   "Yes, yes. But I didn't say we've figured out all the cost implications yet. I know you slipped that one in. Very funny..."

Repeating or paraphrasing what the coachee says is important to verify your understanding, but also to allow the coachee to hear a playback of her thinking and to correct any misunderstanding or misinterpretation.

- ▼ Sounds to me like you're saying...

- ▼ Do I have that right?

- ▼ Let me see if I understand.

- ▼ So you're clear about...? What's not clear is...

- ▼ So you seem to be saying that the goalposts get moved a lot?

- ▼ Am I right in understanding from you that people aren't getting necessary information from other departments?

- ▼ So what you're saying is...

- ▼ So what I'm hearing is that you've been stewing over this for weeks, but you don't know what to do about it, correct?

- ▼ You seem to be saying that this may just be your own opinion. Am I right?

- ▼ Sounds like...

▼ What I'm hearing is that the new office-space plan is creating some turf wars.

_____

_____

_____

FORMULATE A PLAN

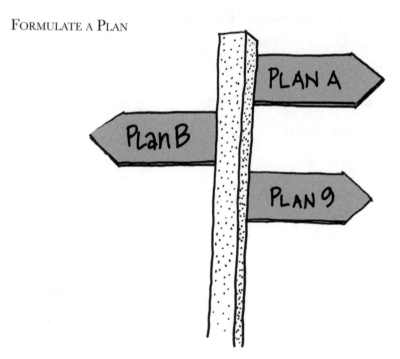

A colleague observed, "A plan is the physical outcome of a coaching session." Motivation is critical to creating a plan and adhering to it. If the coachee isn't motivated, she isn't going to do the heavy lifting that change demands. Once there is commitment, it's time to make a plan. In fact, having a plan helps ensure that the manager/coach maintains the role of collaborator and doesn't become a commanding authority figure. It's fine to define a challenge and problem-solve a solution. But to get from A to J, let alone A to Z, you need a plan. What are the steps and milestones for getting from here to there?

- ▼ What can you do to motivate the team?

- ▼ How comfortable are you with involving your whole team in planning? What's another alternative?

- ▼ Who are the stakeholders here? How do you anticipate getting them on board?

- ▼ Do you have a timetable for this?

- ▼ What small steps are going to get you to this?

- ▼ What do you need to do next time to hit all your targets?

- ▼ What do you need to move this forward?

- ▼ How can you develop your strength in this area?

- ▼ How can you help your team stay on course?

- ▼ Who can make this happen?

- ▼ Do you want to make this a priority right now?

- ▼ What do you want to do next?

- ▼ Who else needs to know what your plans are?

- ▼ What support will you need? From whom?

- ▼ How do you feel about managing this project?

- ▼ Is there someone else you think would be better at the helm?

- ▼ Has anyone on your team taken the company's project management seminar? Would you be interested? Since Henry has already taken it, how do you feel about asking if he could share what he learned?

- ▼ Have you considered working with the team to develop a milestone plan?

Caroline "I was feeling so overwhelmed when you and I talked on Friday about Meg leaving at the end of the month. Everyone's stressed out about it. All those planning meetings coming up. And on top of that, the recruiting process is a total bummer. But our chat got me thinking over the weekend."

Manager "A productive weekend then! So what did you come up with?"

Caroline "I realized that besides losing Meg, who's so terrific, the biggest hassle is bringing her replacement up to speed quickly. We have so much on our plates right now. I've asked Meg to help smooth the transition."

Manager "Good idea. So just to clarify, hiring Meg's replacement now feels doable, given the time constraints?"

Caroline "Yeah. I've delegated that to Mark. He'll do the first round of interviews. Meg's agreed to sit in on the last stage of interviewing and stay on an extra week to help train the newbie and get him or her up to speed."

Manager "Fantastic. Anything else? Any other resources you think could help with this?"

Caroline "Well, actually, I'd love to get HR to fast-track the new hire once we've found our person."

Your coachee might clearly articulate a plan, down to every step and milestone, but that doesn't ensure that she will execute it. Again, motivation is critical. Sometimes, it's a matter of having the necessary resources. Sometimes you yourself, as the manager/coach, could be a critical resource in helping your coachee move ahead. The manager/coach can also help keep the coachee accountable by periodically checking in to see that things are proceeding on track.

▾ Will this move you closer to your goal?

▾ Do you have a clear idea of the steps you need to take?

▾ What are you going to do? When are you going to do it?

▾ Do you want to set milestones? A deadline?

- What are your criteria or measurements for success?

- What obstacles might you encounter, external or internal?

- How can you plan for possible pushback? Then what will you do?

- What could you do differently?

- What support do you need?

- What will you do to obtain that support? When?

- On a scale of one to ten, how real is the plan, as is? How can you make it a ten?

- Now that you know specifically what changes your team has to make, what are you going to do differently to lead them there?

- What do you feel your options are at this point?

- Who else needs to know what your plans are?

- How could you expand your options or go even further with this?

- Are you willing to do what this will take? Including allowing me to help you?

- Do you want to move on this now? How do you feel about taking a wait-and-see approach…maybe until next quarter?

- Is there anything else you want to talk about now before we finish?

Ellen   "Hard to believe just last week I was sitting here all gung-ho to share my research with the finance group at their weekly huddle. I may as well not have gone to the meeting at all."

Manager   "I've been wondering how things went. You were pretty animated about it. Part of your 'stepping up' resolutions."

Ellen   "Yeah, I was psyched after a dry run with my team. But then, Simon launched into his budget presentation as if it were a fait accompli. He just took control. He's the numbers guy—not me."

Manager   "Did he see *your* numbers at all?"

Ellen   "No. I didn't have a chance to present them. Truth is, I could have participated more. I should have participated. I actually believe my projections are more realistic since they are more in tune with the market research."

Manager   "How can you get your findings in front of him?"

Ellen   "What I have should please him—and save his ass. Frankly, I think I'll just ask him for a one-on-one."

Manager   "When are you going to do that?"

Ellen   "I'll see if I can take him to lunch tomorrow."

Manager   "What needs to change when you get with him so you can assure yourself of a better outcome?"

Ellen   "First off, *I'm* buying lunch. And it will be my agenda, totally focused on the research."

Manager   "So, it will be Simon's turn to listen."

Before this conversation, Ellen's manager has coached her on her assertiveness, particularly on taking initiative and following through. Now that Ellen has identified a lost opportunity, her manager encourages her to delve to see how she can salvage this missed occasion to present her numbers. The manager's layered questions are framed to get Ellen to commit to taking the steps she's identified at the lunch she's planning to arrange.

Everyone needs encouragement. Sometimes even a kick in the butt will do. The right question can be a kind of kick in the butt. Often, it's a matter of nailing the coachee down to a commitment to realistic goals and actions. Like motivation, commitment is key. Without it, no significant change is likely to occur. A milestone plan can help. The last question on the following list (How committed are you?) is critical.

▼ Shall we zoom in and get into more detail on this?

▼ How can I help you make it happen?

▼ What could you do to keep yourself juiced?

▼ What has you most excited? How can you build on that excitement?

The power of pluck

"Energy and persistence conquer all things."

Benjamin Franklin

▼ What are you willing to commit to when you do that?

▼ What do you need to do to ensure this happens?

▼ What are your next steps here?

▼ What gets you most excited about this?

▼ Which option(s) will you go for?

▼ To what extent does this meet your objectives?

▼ Still feeling confident about the deadline?

▼ When precisely are you going to start and finish each step?

▼ How can you plan against any obstacles that may arise?

▼ Do you have any last-minute doubts or reservations? What can you do about them?

- ▾ Who else needs to take action here?

- ▾ How committed is everyone?

- ▾ You seem pretty enthusiastic; how committed is the rest of the team? What can you do to get them fired up? What can I do to support you?

- ▾ You're starting on Monday. What can you do to ensure you keep on schedule?

- ▾ How do you feel about this? What might change your feelings?

- ▾ On a one-to-ten scale, how committed are you to make this happen now? (If the answer is less than eight, a flag should go up that there's a major roadblock.) How can you make it a ten?

_____

_____

_____

REVIEW PROGRESS

It's critical to help the coachee identify the learnings and improvements that occur over the course of an initiative. This can happen during the change effort as well as at its culmination. Acknowledging accomplishment (no matter how small) and encouraging a healthy perspective on accomplishment (no matter how small) goes a long way to ensuring that goals are met and enhanced performance is recognized and valued.

- ▼ You really nailed it! What did you do that went well? What did you discover as a result?

- ▼ You were dead on about the pushback from the other departments. How did anticipating this help with the way things played out?

- ▼ How do you feel about the time you invested? What went well? How could you do more of this?

- ▼ Your writing talent really paid off for everyone. How do you feel about raising your hand more often when opportunities like this come up?

- ▼ What impact do you think this had on everyone else? I appreciate your take since it's helpful for me to get a fuller picture of the influence this has had.

- ▼ What was your big take-away this week?

- ▼ What did you learn about yourself that's useful? How could that apply to your role in the upcoming conference?

- ▼ Anywhere else you could leverage this energy?

- ▼ What resources did you have to draw on, internally and externally, to get this done?

- ▼ It's impressive how you stepped up and took control. What helped you do this?

▼ What could have worked better? How can you improve
that on the next go-round?

_____

_____

_____

Topics and Themes

The following questions are grouped according to familiar business-related topics, covering the territory from time management to leadership to communication and more.

These groups of questions also include a selection of themes that may surface in conversation, or that you may choose to introduce because you recognize them as a subtext to what is being said. Emotion, values, and taking action are examples of themes that can be overtly expressed or reveal themselves as an underlying motif that impacts what is being said. Use these more "thematic" threads to frame your dialogue when tackling any of the topic areas suggested here. For example, you could be involved in a discussion centered on time management. There are many time-management questions here. However, in your discussion, you might also want to pursue a line of questioning about values because values relate to the whole subject of how time is or could be better spent.

Justin   "George and I had a productive brainstorming session on the Jessup account. We came up with a clear plan and milestones. It's the best collaborating I think we've done. He got me the projections he said he'd work up for the proposal, and I said I'd incorporate them into some nice-looking charts for the presentation. He was psyched about the whole thing. But now he says he needs the final draft by Friday. I never told him I could deliver it this week. I've got the sales meetings on Tuesday and Wednesday. Thursday we have that IT training session, and I actually have a dental appointment that afternoon."

Justin's words pick up on a prior discussion about communication, but time management surfaces as an issue. The manager who listens carefully can frame his questions in terms of managing time and can cut through a lot of other detail and get to the nub of the frustration Justin is acknowledging.

You get the picture. All these topics and themes cross over each other. It's your job to follow the threads, keep the focus on the challenge (goal), and ask smart, insightful questions as the coaching process moves forward from a goal to a plan, to action, and to maintaining progress. Choose from the following business-related topics and underlying themes to frame your questions. These are lenses you provide as a way to look at behaviors, options, and actions.

VISION OR GOAL

"So where do you see yourself a year from now?"

Some people are clear about the change they want to make. They can describe precisely what they aspire to do and what that will look and feel like when they make it happen. For others, articulating a vision or goal takes some work.

- ▾ Where do you see an opportunity for change?

- ▾ Would it help to make a picture of this? (Suggest a mind map, vision board, or collage.)

- ▾ How do you see making this happen?

- ▾ Can you describe the outcome you envision? How will this impact you? How will this impact the business?

- ▾ If you focus on this, how will things look when you get where you want to go?

- ▾ What could get in the way?

- ▾ What could happen if you gave up on this goal?

- ▾ Perhaps this is no longer relevant to you, an out-of-date dream. What if you let it go? How would that be?

- ▾ Where do you see yourself in three years? Where do you see the organization in three years?

- ▾ What do you want?

- ▾ What would you be thrilled to achieve here?

- ▾ What's your vision of the ideal outcome?

- ▾ If you woke up tomorrow and realized that you had achieved your ideal outcome, how would you know? What would be different? What would be the same?

- ▾ What is the long-term goal related to this issue?

▼ Let's imagine a year or so into the future. What would your ideal work situation be? What would your typical working day look like?

▼ How important is each of these to you? (on a one-to-ten scale?)

Making it real

"Leadership is the capacity to translate vision into reality."

Warren G. Bennis, leading author on leadership

▼ Day-to-day frustrations aside, what is it about your work that gives you the most satisfaction? The most dissatisfaction?

▼ What lies behind the dissatisfaction? What could erase that concern?

▼ How much of your time at work do you feel positive? How much negative? Let's look at the positive.

▼ What options do you have for changing things? What would be the benefits of doing that? What would you lose?

▼ What position do you aspire to? How can you get there?

▼ So changing position or going independent are two options. How could you apply some of the attractions of each of these options to what you're doing now?

▼ How else? Where? And where else?

▼ What would you have to change? What could you do to change that? Who could you ask to have other parts changed?

▼ If you were able to change all those parts, how well would your needs be met?

▼ What are your greatest needs? Wants? Why?

VALUES

Most of the actions we take are driven by our values. However, we're not always in touch with which values are driving our actions. Is it autonomy? Collaboration? Fun? Honesty? Integrity? Leadership? Loyalty? We don't often identify the values that motivate us or realize how they can be tapped as part of an effort to change. Coaching can help connect someone to this personal bottom line in a given situation, particularly as it impacts job performance. A manager/coach needs to be in touch with his own values and biases to be an effective guide in conversations about values. This is not about judging values, but clarifying them.

Values shopping

"We can tell our values by looking at our checkbook stubs."

Gloria Steinem

- ▾ How is that important to you?

- ▾ When did that matter?

- ▾ Where does it show up consistently?

- ▾ Which values show up?

- ▾ Are your actions aligned with your values?

- ▾ What's standing in the way?

- ▾ Where do you feel the most energy?

- ▾ What inspires you?

- Who inspires you?

- Do you have a role model? Who is it? Explain how she is a role model.

- What values does she reflect?

- What sort of people and activities do you enjoy most at work?

- What is it about those people and activities that you most like?

- What qualities do they represent? Where else do you find these qualities?

- What activities in or out of work are meaningful to you?

- How would you like to be remembered as a colleague (or teammate or leader)?

- How do your core values differentiate you from your colleagues?

- How do your values show up in your decision making?

- What gives that importance for you?

- What do you think will matter to you in five years? Ten years?

- What impact do you want to have?

- This is important to you because ...

_____

_____

_____

Manager	"So Jake's constant sniping at you is an issue. What's at stake for you here?"
Tamara	"Nothing major. He hasn't actually stabbed me in the back yet, but it's annoying."
Manager	"You say it's not a major issue, but it's annoying enough that you've raised it with me. Have you had any other thoughts about how to handle this?"
Tamara	"I could address it with him head on..."
Manager	"How do you think he'll react?"
Tamara	"I'm guessing he'll appreciate the candor and directness. He's a pretty no-nonsense sort of guy."
Manager	"So how do you plan to introduce this?"
Tamara	"I could take him out of the office... for lunch."
Manager	"Neutral ground. Sounds wise. And broaching the issue? I mean, are you going to wait for dessert?"
Tamara	"Ha, ha, good point. I need to be clear on timing. I do know he wouldn't want to feel it's a setup. So I'll let him know when I invite him that there's something I'd like to discuss."

Some people avoid conflict at all costs, even giving in on positions important to them. More headstrong types often jump into contentious exchanges without considering alternatives to bumping heads.

Conflict is about interpersonal relations, which, of course, involve individual behavior. What's in the way? Lack of empathy? Insecurity? (Even Type A managers have insecurities!) Coaching offers an opportunity to recognize how one deals with conflict (self-awareness) and to explore options for handling disagreement and how these steps could make things better (motivation). Coaching around conflict issues places emphasis on understanding the conflict, gaining insight, and identifying proactive steps that can be taken to improve the situation.

- ▼ How do you envision addressing this uncomfortable situation?

- ▼ What's another way you could introduce the topic?

- ▼ How might you approach it, considering what's at stake?

- ▼ Do you notice any patterns in your own behavior when you find yourself in disagreement?

- ▼ What is your usual response to conflict? How has that worked for you?

- ▼ What ideas or goals have you fought for in recent years?

- ▼ What have you gone to the mat for? How did you do that?

- ▼ What can you do to get her buy-in?

- ▼ Have you considered her point of view?

- ▼ Have you asked him his opinion on this?

- ▼ What kind of input is he most responsive to? Most resistant to?

_____

_____

_____

Manager "We spoke last month about getting the three departments to collaborate better. How's that working out?"

Nathaniel "I did have a discussion with the VPs as I said I would. Melinda is with me on this—quite gung-ho, actually. Sam is this way, that way, and basically doesn't know how he feels about it. But Leonard is flat out against the whole idea. Getting commitment here is going to be tough!"

Manager "It's good you followed through and met with everyone. At least you introduced a goal to pursue with them."

Nathaniel "The question is whether this is going to move beyond that introduction."

Manager "So I'm hearing this is going to be tougher than you thought. What's the difficulty here, as you see it?"

Nathaniel "Sam and Leonard are the bottlenecks. I think Sam is threatened by change, and Leonard is protecting his turf and his way of working. They don't see why they should change anything."

Manager "So what could be one step toward their doing things differently?"

Nathaniel "I'm thinking it's time to invite the division president, get everybody in one room, and have him paint the big picture of where we need to go. With a little senior push, Melinda, Leonard, and Sam can hopefully work out their common goals and ways we can all successfully meet them...beyond business as usual."

Manager "Sounds good. What's the next step?"

Change is inevitable, but that doesn't make it easy. Coaching can help someone anticipate change and plan for it. It can provide the necessary support throughout the process, making it smoother and more likely to succeed for all involved.

A "change"ing mindset

"If you believe that people hate change and that it is your job to change them, they will hate it.

If you believe that people thrive on change and that your job is to unleash it, you will tap into a limitless source of ingenuity, energy, and drive that will allow you to consistently take your big ideas into big results."

Michael T. Kanazawa
www.changethis.com

- What's your usual response to change? Do you welcome it?

- How do you feel about the reorg? What's clear? What's unclear?

- What's working? What's not working?

- What are you hearing from your team about the restructuring? What are you noticing?

- How are you preparing your people? Is there pushback? How are you dealing with that?

- Have you planned for pushback? From whom?

- Since your departments have merged, have you noticed any effective new work styles? How can you make them permanent?

- What new skills are you looking for in hiring his replacement?

- What's your priority in considering this new hire?

- How's the new hire working out?

- What are your long-term plans for her?

- What are her plans? How do you see these lining up?

- Considering the budget situation, what else could you do, short of hiring a new person?

- What other resources could you use...besides duct tape? Any untapped capacity out there?

- How is the move affecting you?

- ▼ Whose support do you have? How is he supporting you? Is there someone else you could reach out to?

- ▼ Is there any way you can take advantage of the extra commute time?

- ▼ With your new space, how's the noise? How are you handling the fishbowl aspect of the open office? What could you do about this?

PERFORMANCE REVIEW

"Before we get to my review, I was wondering if this is a good time to ask for a raise."

Coaching can be an important part of a performance review. However, at the end of the day, the manager must communicate what's working and what needs improvement. That said, businesses often grapple with setting clear performance criteria and with the performance-review process itself. Expectations aren't always clear or consistent. The entire experience can involve unnecessary stress, resentment, and dissension. Using a coaching style in managing your people can give you an edge in setting goals and reviewing performance. Coaching techniques can help make the process fair and accurate, and ensure that all parties benefit from the insights and perceptions expressed, whether it's a first-time review or one for a person with a long history with the company.

- ▼ How useful do you think performance reviews are?

- ▼ What do you find challenging about reviews?

- ▼ What have you learned from the reviews you've had?

- ▼ What important criteria should be part of your review?

- ▼ Where shall we have your review this year, my office or yours?

- ▼ Is there anyone whose input you'd like to include whom you'd like me to talk to?

- ▼ Do you want to add any points you want to address in your review?

- ▼ What has been really working? Where are there gaps? What can you do to get past this roadblock?

- ▼ So how would you grade yourself on that? What's your thinking here? How could you make this a ten?

- ▼ How can we talk about this in a way that works toward a solution?

- ▼ Who could help you? What do you need?

- ▼ What did you want to discuss about a raise?

- ▼ What I'd like to do is focus on how best to help you fulfill your potential in your role, if that's something you're interested in.

- ▼ What's the biggest insight you've had from what's happened?

- ▼ So, things haven't gone as well as you wanted? What do you need to focus on, moving ahead?

- ▼ Great, so you hit all your goals. How can you run with this?

- ▼ What have you learned from this whole situation?

- ▼ Is there anything more I could do to make this review process more useful for you?

EMOTIONS

Adam	"Lisa's got so much energy. She only recently came on board; and already at this week's meeting, she dove right into the budget. I mean, she said she's not a numbers person, but she asked great questions and cut through a lot of the usual crap we go through over the projections."
Manager	"You seem pretty energized too. Glad to hear she's having such an impact. How does the rest of the group feel about her?"
Adam	"Folks are pretty happy the meetings aren't dragging on as usual. Maybe they're just as long, but she's definitely raised the fun factor. And she delivers on what she promises. At least so far..."
Manager	"You really sound up about the influence she's having. How can you leverage her energy?"
Adam	"Hmmm. I think I'll recommend her for the management-training program coming up next month."
Manager	"What else might you do?"
Adam	"I could invite her to sit in on some client meetings."

Addressing emotions in a coaching context can offer real traction. We all operate in some emotional context. Conscious or not, emotions play into behaviors in a big way. Emotions inform perceptions, attitudes, and decisions in ways that can have a major impact on business, both for good and for not so good. This goes for the manager as well as the coachee. So it's important for a manager/coach to have a good grip on her own emotions. That said, here's a rule of thumb for discussing emotions in a business context: the manager/coach should be clear on boundaries—keep the discussion focused on the business domain, not the private and personal realm. There are gray areas between the two, and the coach should be comfortable going into them, so long as they help lead back to the business challenge. Coaching helps people recognize and validate feelings and encourages them to use their emotions in ways that benefit them and the business.

- ▼ You're smiling a lot. What's going on?

- ▼ What are you going to do with all this positive energy?

- ▼ What can you do to sustain this energy?

- ▼ How are you holding up with all the layoffs?

- ▼ What feels most challenging here?

- ▼ How did that sit with you?

- ▼ What can you do to relieve the stress?

- ▼ When do you feel most stressed? Is there a pattern that you see?

- ▼ When do you feel the most relaxed? Is there a pattern here?

- ▼ What can you take from those relaxed moments and capture in those stressful ones?

- ▼ What can you do to stay calm in the moment?

- ▼ Is there someone you can share these feelings with who could offer an outside perspective?

- ▼ Are you taking care of yourself well enough? What could you do better?

- ▼ How is this influencing your attitude? Your stress levels?

- ▼ How do you feel about risk? When might taking a risk be a good thing? When is it questionable?

- ▼ How does your hesitancy play out? What's the impact? What could you do to feel more comfortable with asserting yourself? What else?

Team Building

Julia   "I sent out the announcement for this year's team retreat. I feel like a short-order cook dealing with everyone's requests. No surprise, Rob wants us all to go snowboarding!"

Manager   "I recall hearing that wasn't a big hit last year. What are other issues you're hearing about?"

Julia   "Nina has special dietary needs. Ray seems pretty apathetic about the whole thing. He was miserable with the activities last year. The ropes course almost did him in. I just don't have time to sort it all out..."

Manager   "Isn't Mike a vegetarian? How did that work out before?"

Julia   "Good point. I had him speak to the caterers beforehand. I should suggest he help Nina with food requirements. Not sure about Ray, though. He always seems happy to stay on the sidelines and bury his nose in a crossword."

Manager   "But you want Ray to be on board with the plans, right?"

Julia   "Of course! We always need him to ride shotgun and navigate on the road, for one. He loves maps and really gets into piloting us around!"

Manager   "How else could he participate?"

Julia   "This might seem a bit left-field, but I could get him together with Rob to come up with some ideas for making this year's retreat more interesting—short of snowboarding! Maybe the two of them can come up with some new activities, figure out the logistics, and get back to the others."

Manager   "Team building before the team building! Good for you. Maybe they'll suggest some sledding and hypoallergenic snacks with sudoku challenges after the slopes."

Simply grouping people together doesn't make them a team. Supporting, empowering, motivating, and engaging them with respect and open communication is what develops a team. The listening and questioning you do in the coaching conversations you have with your people will enhance your leadership and your success in building your team and helping your teammates build their own teams.

- ▼ How much of your time do you devote to the team? To the individuals on the team? Does this seem to be the right balance?

- ▼ How well do you feel you know the people you work with? Their learning styles? Their communication styles?

- ▼ How well is your team balanced in terms of strengths, work styles, communications styles? Where are there gaps or overlaps? How could those be accommodated?

- ▼ What factors come into play with the people on your team?

- ▼ Have you noticed any biases or particular values you have that affect your work or the work environment? How do these impact things?

- ▼ How much do you trust your people (on a one-to-ten scale)? How much do they trust you? What could happen to improve that trust? What could you do?

Team Building

- ▼ How important is it to you that you get everyone's input?

- ▼ How do you invite input? What else do you do?

- ▼ Whose input is most important? Why?

- ▼ How do you know everyone is being heard and has an opportunity to weigh in?

- ▼ What are your values? How do they impact your expectations of yourself? Of your team?

- ▼ How important is the fun factor for you? For your colleagues?

- ▼ Can you point to what contributes to your successful meetings?

- How do you typically go about making a decision? When do you include others in your decision making?

- Do you acknowledge your people? How? When?

- Do you listen well? How do you know you do? How could you improve your listening?

- Are you comfortable collaborating? Co-creating?

- How do you balance control and delegation?

- What could happen if you gave more responsibility to your people? If you opened up the problem solving and decision making more?

TIME MANAGEMENT

Dana "The time-management matrix you suggested was a real eye opener. I could actually see on paper that so many things I think are urgent really aren't."

Manager "So, what did you learn about where you spend most of your time?"

Dana "One thing's for sure. I spend the least amount of time on me."

Manager "What does that tell you?"

Dana "It's no surprise I'm always wrestling with the extra pounds and resenting not using my vacation time. I feel like I'm working on fumes."

Manager "Where do you think you *can* find time for yourself?"

Dana "For starters, I'd like to cut down on unnecessary meetings. Some of the stuff we discuss endlessly could probably be handled differently. Like updates. The team spends so much time reporting. I could ask Chuck to collapse all the reports into one summary report to present to the group."

Manager	"You've said it might be good for Chuck to take on more responsibility."
Dana	"I *did* say that, didn't I? Giving Chuck more authority could also be great for me—and my stress levels, just watching the clock. That could mean saving an hour a week. We might even be able to finish our meetings earlier. Would that be okay?"
Manager	"Certainly sounds like a possibility. How do think that might change things?"
Dana	"Fewer interruptions, less stress, and more concentrated time for the annual report layout—my magnum opus!"
Manager	"Definitely a start. What else can you give up or delegate?"

There may be only so many hours in the day, but it's easy to lose track of them. Remember the kids who always got their homework in early and coolly showed up on time for every sports practice? But what about those frazzled souls who showed up late with homework pages missing, then sped off to practice, arriving after the scrimmage was already under way?

Many of us find ourselves somewhere between those extremes, grappling with the clock and trying to manage our time before it gets away from us. Coaching can help us take a hard look at how we spend our time. Further, addressing issues involving lateness (such as showing up late to meetings or missing deadlines) will most likely introduce the need to learn to say no, to better delegate, to prioritize, to give up some things. As a

Where did the time go?

Email
How much time do you spend on email? How could you cut that in half?

Meetings
How much time do you spend in meetings? How much of that is not necessary? How could that business be handled differently?

Plan
Do you work according to a plan? How could making a work plan save time?

Interruptions
How could carving out a solid hour a day without phone calls or other interruptions make a difference?

Clutter
What does your desk look like? How might uncluttering your desk and office impact your work? Could you translate this change into time saved?

manager/coach you can take advantage of a variety of time-management tools as you work with your coachee. Many can be found online, including Stephen Covey's Time Management Matrix and his Circles of Concern and Influence.

▼ Where do you spend most of your time?

▼ What are your major time wasters?

▼ How do you evaluate what needs to be done now? How do you prioritize?

▼ Are there patterns to these decisions? How do they serve you?

▼ If you're consistently late, what's in that for you?

▼ Do you like being too busy? What does that offer you?

▼ Can you say no to things? How can you say no when you need to?

▼ What's not getting done that is really important?

▼ Is there anyone you could delegate that to? How would that sit with you?

▼ What could you delegate?

▼ How can you become more effective?

▼ Can you see advantages to bringing in a consultant to work with the team?

▼ Have you done any milestone planning? Would that prove helpful?

▼ How is the milestone plan working?

▼ Is that schedule doable? What could make it more real?

- ▼ What needs to change to assure you that you can deliver the project on time?

- ▼ What do you need to meet the deadline? People? Resources?

LEADERSHIP DEVELOPMENT

Monica "I've let myself down. I simply didn't step up when I had the chance."

Manager "What do you mean by 'step up'?"

Monica "I didn't take charge of the group in our planning session and move the agenda forward. It seemed like everyone was talking at once. But by the time I acknowledged that we were getting nowhere, we only had an hour left to create the first-pass blueprint for the new product line. Basically, the meeting didn't generate any exciting ideas."

Manager "What can you do about this now?"

Monica "We're meeting again tomorrow, and I've told everyone we absolutely have to deliver."

Manager "What can you do to fire up the team?"

Monica "I could begin the meeting by owning the fact that I virtually threw water on things and didn't really encourage their creative mojo. I'll try to jump-start things by being clearer about our goal too. I think we lost sight of this. I saw this great *New Yorker* – ish cartoon last week. It had a bunch of dogs talking to one another. One dialog balloon had a T-bone, another a Frisbee, another had a squirrel, another was...well, you get the picture. I think I'll email it ahead and say I'm looking forward to hearing their ideas and having a lively brainstorming session."

Manager "Sounds like you're stepping up. What else can you do to kick off the meeting, really get the ball rolling, then stay on course so you all come away satisfied?"

In this exchange, Monica is demonstrating self-awareness and humility, which help her change course to get buy-in from her team and have a productive planning session. Leadership is the most significant hallmark of a successful manager. Endless books, papers, webinars, and conferences focus on leadership. Rock-star corporate leaders regularly appear on magazine covers. It's important that managers not only seek to gain leadership skills they may not have but also recognize and develop the ones they do. A manager/coach's feedback can also help in this regard ("I've observed…Do you agree?"). Good feedback encourages the coachee to go to the next level.

▼ Is there a difference between being a manager and being a leader? Can you explain how you see that?

▼ What leadership strengths do you feel you bring to your role?

▼ How do you communicate your vision to your people? Do they share it?

▼ Can you visualize the desired outcome? What do you have to do to get there? Can you communicate this clearly?

▼ What impact are you having on people? What impact do you want to have?

▼ What are you doing to get people on board? How's the response?

▼ What more could you do? Any other ideas?

▼ What are you doing to develop your people?

▼ What else could you do?

▼ What kind of feedback have you been getting that you've found helpful? How has that impacted what you do?

▼ What's missing? Where are the gaps in your own performance?

▼ What actions can you take to generate more collaboration?

- Does your team see you as a positive role model? Do you see yourself walking the talk?

- What can you let go of that could free up more of your time? Where will you spend it?

- What have you learned about your leadership style?

- What is it that only you can do? Why do you feel that way?

- What do you do to reenergize yourself? What could you do now?

> **Ladies first!**
>
> "Only one man in a thousand is a leaderof men—the other 999 follow women."
>
> *Groucho Marx*

- Do you want to take a closer look at how you're managing your time?

- What do you feel comfortable sharing? Uncomfortable? With whom? Under what circumstances?

- How is your preference to keep things close to the vest impacting your people's performance?

- What's a first step you could take to make your decision making more transparent?

- Have your actions ever surprised anyone? How so? What expectations do people have of you?

- What is your attitude toward risk? How is that?

- What have you done to provide your people the room to fail? What about you…have you challenged the status quo recently?

- What have you done to build trust among your people? How can you take that further?

See also "Values" questions (p. 76).

_____

_____

_____

Talent Development and Succession

Every one of us needs to feel we are valued and that our contributions make a difference. However, we often delude ourselves into believing we're indispensable—that no one can take our place. Not so. Everyone can be replaced. A hard lesson, for sure. Still, to the extent we can have impact in helping groom potential candidates for moving up (even into *our* present position), we should seize the opportunity. That means growing the skills and competencies of the promising talent whom we manage.

The core of a manager's job is to develop her people. This includes identifying people with high potential to advance in the organization. Coaching related to talent development introduces opportunities to tap hidden capabilities, develop and expand skills, assemble high-performing teams, manage/risk, and, in particular, plan for succession (within the team).

- ▼ What does "high potential" mean to you?

- ▼ Historically, where are your best sources of high-potential people?

- ▼ How are you identifying and developing future leaders for the highest-level positions in the company?

- ▼ Are you clear about expectations with your people?

- ▼ Does your team have the resources they need to do their best work? How can that be improved?

- ▼ How much of your time do you yourself spend actively developing your people? How?

- ▼ Do you regularly acknowledge your people and their progress? How?

- ▼ Do you welcome criticism and input?

- ▼ How do you define leadership? How else?

- ▼ How did you come to understand leadership this way?

- ▼ What are the leadership strengths that you feel are integral to your role?

- ▼ How can those be cultivated in the people you've identified as successor material?

- ▼ What specific skill sets are integral to your work? How are you developing those in your people?

- What do you know about a plan for succession in the company? Is it meeting expectations? How could it be improved?

- Do you have thoughts about a succession process that everyone could be committed to?

- What do you think is needed to create a succession plan? Who do you believe should be involved?

ALIGNMENT

Peter   "I suppose you heard the meetings with the client were dismal. They nixed the new packaging concept."

Manager   "What did you learn?"

Peter   "Besides the fact that they are the client from hell?"

Manager   "No, really. What surprised you most about their rejecting what you guys presented?"

Peter   "Basically, they feel the colors and imaging are too similar to the preschool line. This infant line is geared toward the mother as purchaser."

Manager   "And what did you do to accommodate that?"

Peter   "Not much. In thinking back, Marcus did suggest we get more testimonials and put them right on the box. And Lydia thought that photos of the mom or dad with the baby, rather than just the baby alone, would be more compelling."

Manager   "You seem to be suggesting that Marcus and Lydia were on to something. Any take-aways from this?"

Peter	"I think I didn't realize how much ownership I felt, having come up with the concept for the original line when we launched the brand. I was so locked into a one-size-fits-all solution. This is a totally different offering. I should have responded to the client's signals. It's their business. They know their market. And Marcus and Lydia were much more customer-focused."
Manager	"Where do you go from here?"
Peter	"We promised another go-round with some thumbnail designs by next week."
Manager	"What else could you do to be sure everyone's on the same page this time?"
Peter	"Wheels turning...I could suggest we have a prep session with their product development team before we move ahead."
Manager	"When will you arrange for that?"
Peter	"As soon as I get back to my office."
Manager	"Onward!"

Coaching can be an effective tool in aligning individual action with team, business, and client goals. And coaching conversations can reveal inconsistencies and miscommunication. Acknowledging and exploring these gaps can help reveal the source of employees' frustration, missed deadlines, or even unhappy customers. Moreover, solutions can be worked out to ensure those involved are working off the same script. Alignment between the manager/coach and coachee is the foundation for a successful coaching experience. If there is mutual understanding and agreement on the determined goal, plan, and action, it is more likely that the action will be successful.

▾ What makes you feel that your team is working at cross-purposes? How could this be avoided?

▾ How can you work with him to ensure he stays on track?

▾ What can you do to ensure your group is clearer on what's going on with the product development group?

▾ How can you keep communication lines open?

▼ How will the cutbacks impact your needs? How can you accommodate these changes?

▼ How did you develop your milestone plan? Did you all do it as a team? And how can you set up a control system that will guarantee everyone is on the same page when it comes to meeting your milestones?

▼ What additional information or resources could your team use? How do you know?

▼ If you could get the company to take steps to better communicate this year's budget strategy and product development plans, what would those be?

▼ What can you do to contribute to these improvements? Who else could have an impact? How do you see that playing out?

▼ Overall, where do you think there could be more transparency in the company?

▼ What do you think about the company's mission as stated? Do you support it? How do your people feel about it?

▼ How does your group's plan line up with the company's new mission statement? Do you need to adjust your plan?

▼ How is your work impacted by the overall mission and strategy?

▼ How's your weekly check-in with the client working out? Where do you see room for improvement?

▼ Is there another person on the customer side you feel you should have regular contact with?

- ▼ Where are we falling short of their expectations? What can we do to remedy this?

_____

_____

_____

Communication (internal and external)

Regina "Jackie mentioned you weren't happy with my department's presentation last week."

Liz "To be honest, I wasn't."

Regina "Would now be a good time to talk about it?"

Liz "Sure."

Regina "So what didn't work for you?"

Liz "It was as if you never received our projections. Your department didn't acknowledge Rita's research, and then you all barreled ahead with the sales strategy. It seemed like you didn't consider the new market research at all."

Regina "We get so siloed here sometimes. OK, I own that one. I should have gone into detail with my people and discussed all your findings up front. You're right, but I'm sure we can turn this around."

Liz "And I should have come to you before going to Jackie. Could have avoided this misunderstanding."

Regina "I can take the criticism, no problem. But tell me, what else could help us steer clear of these misfired messages?"

Liz "Perhaps you could send out the meeting agendas ahead of time. For my part, I can scoot you an email with any points I think should be included."

Regina "Sounds good. Anything else?"

This is an example of peer-to-peer coaching. In this instance, Regina initiates a conversation with Liz in an effort to address head-on a point of dissatisfaction between their teams. Regina's open-ended questions and acknowledgment of her own communication failings open the way for her and Liz to clarify things and set up protocols to avoid future misunderstandings, achieve stronger buy-in for all stakeholders in the work at hand, and deliver better business results.

> ## Listening is communicating too.
>
> "The key to success is to get out into the store and listen to what the associates have to say. It's terribly important for everyone to get involved. Our best ideas come from clerks and stock boys."
>
> *Sam Walton*

Openness, clarity, and careful listening can help avoid those all too familiar excuses—"If only I'd known," "I had no idea," "You never told me that," "He never said that"—that result from noncommunication and miscommunication. Managers set the tone and help define and model the organization's culture. Unfortunately, open communication is often the exception rather than the rule. It takes awareness and sensitivity to different styles of communication and real commitment to establish a culture of clear and ongoing exchange that can ensure better understanding of the work at hand and expectations for performance. Issues surrounding communication often surface in coaching conversations.

- ▼ How would you describe your communication style?

- ▼ Would you describe yourself as more directive or more collaborative? How is that working out for you? What do you notice about people's reactions?

- ▼ Are you comfortable with how you communicate? Can you talk more about that? When have things gone well? What can you take from that?

- ▼ Do you actively invite feedback? How?

▼ What kind of feedback do you get? What kind of feedback do you give? How is your feedback received?

▼ How important to you is acknowledging your people's achievement? How do you do it? How could you improve on that?

▼ How do you feel when you have to deliver difficult news? What can you do to make it easier for yourself and still get the message across?

▼ In a conversation, how important is listening for you? Do you mostly listen in your conversations? How does it affect people's performance?

▼ How could you improve your listening?

▼ How is everyone getting on? In what ways are things breaking down? How have you addressed this? What's been the response?

▼ What could you do to get her to play ball? How can you enlist the others?

▼ If you could imagine a better communication pipeline between your departments, how would that work?

▼ How isolated is your group feeling? Are there some walls that could be taken down? How could this help?

▼ How informed are people about the other business units? About the big-picture plans for the company and their status? What could you see happening to create more transparency?

_____

_____

_____

"As I was saying,..."

There's a big difference between going through the motions, even if the job gets done, and bringing curiosity and passion to the work. Engaged employees deliver and grow in the process of delivering. Companies with high levels of employee engagement are proven to be more successful. Effective managers understand this and actively seek to recognize their people's strengths and give them challenging opportunities to excel.

Managers need to have antennae for people who are undermotivated and help infuse excitement and meaning into the work. Managers need to make clear that what particular employees are doing is aligned with others on the team, with their department, and with where the business wants to go (see "Alignment," p. 98). Often, it's a matter of discussing how the "whole is more than the sum of its parts." That is, conveying how an individual's work contributes to other parts of the business or to a finished project to which the employee has no direct exposure.

Appreciation and acknowledgment certainly play an important role in fostering engagement. Coaching itself can be instrumental in helping engage someone in his work, with his team, and in his own professional development.

- ▼ How important is this project to you? What interests you the most? What is missing?

- ▼ Is something simply not working? What could draw you in more? How would that look?

- ▼ Is there something I can do?

- ▼ Is there something else you'd rather be working on? What would that offer you?

- ▼ What can you offer that we haven't tapped?

- ▼ How invested in this presentation is the team? How do you feel about it?

- ▼ Is there someone you'd like to pull in on this?

- ▼ You were all gung-ho to work on this; now, not so. What's changed?

- ▼ What could turn things around for you?

- ▼ Is there something else going on that's distracting you?

- ▼ When have you been most involved in your work? What made that happen? What could you do now to approach that satisfaction and involvement?

_____

_____

_____

Work-Life Balance

Roger   "I know we have this hard deadline with the Abbott forecast, and we need all hands on deck."

Manager   "Yeah...?"

Roger   "But it's hard for me to be here sixty hours a week with my dad now living with us since his fall."

Manager   "You're right, we do need to get this project delivered on schedule, but it sounds like you're having a tough time of it. How is that impacting things?"

Roger   "Well, it's slowing things down. It's been a huge distraction, and I'm really tired."

Manager   "Let's forget the Abbott forecast for a minute. What's the forecast for your dad?"

Roger   "We're waiting for a bed to open up in this rehab center, which should be sometime in the next two weeks. Then two weeks after that, they'll provide part-time care for him at his place. It's really a temporary situation."

Manager   "Sounds like you've arranged things pretty well, and your dad is on the road to recovery. So his living with you is a short-term situation. What are some options here to keep things moving along?"

Roger   "When I think about it, I realize I've been micromanaging a lot. Sonia is always telling me to let go a bit—at least let her handle the client communication. I should take her advice!"

Manager   "How confident are you that she can manage that?"

Roger   "Very. That's pretty much what she did in her previous job. This would free up at least a couple of hours for me on Tuesday and Friday mornings, which I could use to handle some of my dad's medical stuff."

Manager   "Sounds doable. Any other time-saving ideas?"

Roger   "Abbott needs the project done, but I do think we could submit a draft a week before deadline to get their feedback...it could be 99 percent there. If they have changes, that might buy us another few days."

Manager   "So, you *have* options. Is there anything else you can do to ease the load and still keep close to schedule?"

Roger "I was also thinking, since there are no meetings scheduled until the fifteenth, I could easily work from home for the next week. That might save revising the deadline too."

Manager "Go for it."

Work-life balance issues are often front and center and must be addressed head on. Often, these issues are disguised as something else. The fact is, our twenty first-Century lives are packed with to-do lists and unending responsibilities and stress. Managing time in both professional and private spheres and finding a way to balance both are a constant challenge. Some people manage better than others. By addressing this area holistically, coaching can help identify whether this balance is the underlying issue.

Coaching conversations can trigger thinking about how to navigate between professional and private worlds in a way that brings greater satisfaction in each. But, like emotions, work-life balance is sensitive stuff, and the manager/coach needs to be prepared for where such conversations can lead. Boundaries are important. The coach needs to recognize when the content moves too far into the private domain and out of the coach's area of expertise. At times like that, a referral to a mental health professional might be in order.

- ▼ How are you feeling about the hours you're putting in on this project?

- ▼ So, you've got some personal stuff you need to take care of. What can we do to help you juggle things?

- ▼ What resources would you need to get both things moving forward?

- ▼ Is the deadline realistic? Is it adjustable?

- ▼ What can you delegate here at work?

- ▼ Can you delegate some things on the home front?

- ▼ Who would be willing to lend a hand temporarily?

- ▼ How much of your work each week could be accomplished from home?

- ▼ What's doable? What's not doable?

- ▼ What's negotiable at this point? What's not negotiable?

- ▼ Is there something you can give up here? At home?

- ▼ How can you cut back on the work you're taking home and still meet your deadlines?

- ▼ Can you work during your commute?

- ▼ What can I do to help take the pressure off?

_____

_____

_____

Asking: What's the big idea?

No wonder coaches speak of "powerful questioning." Incisive questions used to a strategic purpose can truly generate those "Aha!" moments. Those are the revelations that can critically influence growth and change and enhance individual and business performance. When you make the effort to guide the conversational process with a successful outcome in mind, you are enhancing your own performance as a manager, leader, and critical player in the success of the business

"What could happen if you do nothing?"

3. Suggesting

Suggesting puts another option on the table.

In a coaching conversation, the goal of suggesting is to offer the benefit of some added options that you can put on the table

From on high

"The Ten Commandments were not a suggestion."

Pat Riley
past coach of L.A. Lakers

Suggestions can be powerful. They are, after all, just that—**suggestions—ideas, possible plans, or actions for someone to *consider*.** They are not direct orders or prescriptions.

Suggesting is another way of guiding the process of change. It's the coachee, after all, who makes the decision and does the changing.

There's a difference between *suggesting* ("Have you considered using some vacation days?") and *advising* ("You should use some of your vacation days"). Suggestions should follow the direction of the coachee's thinking.

Have you considered...?

A survey of participants who were coached during executive education programs revealed that managers wanted their coach to make action recommendations.

Robert Hooiberg and Nancy Lane
International Institute for Management
Development (IMD)

As manager, if you have something useful to offer, you can introduce it for deliberation. You can also ask permission first: "Would you like a suggestion from me?"

Beware of doing the work for your coachees—don't do their thinking for them or give them the answers. That's why suggesting something in a coaching conversation *can* be tricky. It needs to be done in a way that doesn't interrupt the coachee's own thinking and ideation. It needs to be introduced in the context of the conversation, that is, as organically as possible. Whatever you suggest should relate to something the coachee has said, or perhaps not said. Suggestions are tools for the coachee to use to expand her own thinking and allow her to own the actions she decides to take.

Suggestions are us

The New York City – based collaborative Illegal Art hauled an enormous white suggestion box to each of the city's five boroughs to collect suggestions from passers-by. What they collected ran the gamut: "Love each other or perish." "Take breath mints when offered." "Give me a break!" "More time in the day." By the Brooklyn Bridge, a woman misspelled her message memorably: "Never brake up with someone on a bridge." Over 350 entries and 50 photos appear in *Suggestion*, the book based on this person-on-the-street collaboration.

Suggesting is the third building block of the coaching conversation model, an integral element in your dialogues as a manager coaching your people. After all, you likely have expertise and experience related to whatever specific challenges they are facing. Suggestions represent another opportunity to demonstrate your command of the situation, offer your own insights, and leverage your knowledge as a leader in opening your people's field of vision.

When to suggest

Timing is everything. It's your job as manager/coach to recognize when an opportunity to make a suggestion presents itself—to be "in the moment" and respond with your input. Sometimes, on reflection, an option may occur to you that will fit better in a subsequent conversation. Before you weigh in with your suggestion, be sure the coachee has exhausted her own store of possible options or ideas.

Often, when someone says, "It's just a suggestion," it can sound loaded or disingenuous. You don't want to sound like a crazy uncle who's always offering unsolicited advice. A suggestion is best offered when you're not concerned about its being rejected and not too attached to the outcome (that is, when you're able to take your ego out of the game). While your suggestion might prove useful to you or the business, the critical thing is its potential for being useful to your coachee.

You can use suggestions to

- ▼ Generate energy and action

- ▼ Jump-start new thinking

- ▼ Enhance an action plan

- ▼ Offer another point of view

Emma	"I'm sick of the same old PowerPoint graphics. Borrrrrinngg."
Manager	"I know what you mean. There are just so many bulleted lists we can look at before all we see are dots and letters. What are you thinking about doing for this presentation?"
Emma	"At last year's conference, I took a bunch of photos of folks from all the divisions. I thought of incorporating them somehow to make everyone feel represented and bring home the message of 'integrated solutions,' which of course is this year's theme. But right now, I'm just sitting on a lot of pictures. Not sure what to do with them."
Manager	"Have you had *any* ideas?"
Emma	"Just putting them into the PowerPoint, matching people with their business units as we review each unit's plans for the upcoming year."
Manager	"Anything else you could do with the pictures?"
Emma	"I'm feeling a bit stuck. I feel there *should* be more I could do. Everyone on the team seems to be counting on me to produce the PowerPoint. They all have enough on their plates to get ready for the conference."
Manager	"Have you considered interviewing some of the pictured people about the conference topic?"
Emma	"Wow. I hadn't thought of that...an 'in their own words' perspective. That could really add so much to the photos. Hmmm, I could see recording them, if they're OK with that. Maybe Mark could help me edit some sound bites to use as a track with the slides. He has a mini recording studio set up at his band's rehearsal space. We could do it there. Thanks, this is great."
Manager	"Any other options if you get pushback on the interviews?"
Emma	"I think folks will be amenable, but I suppose I can always ask for suggestions. I'm reaching out to everyone anyway."

Sometimes, we all get stuck in our thinking. We can visit something for what seems like umpteen times and consider solutions over and over, and still feel like there is something missing or we have nowhere else to go. When a person is stuck in a "brain freeze," a little input from someone else can go a long way to greasing those thinking wheels. When you're really listening and working to encourage your coachee to come up with solutions, ideas are likely to come to you. Sometimes, they will surprise you because it just might be your gut instinct that generates suggestions. Sometimes you may consciously draw on your own experience.

Audience participation

"I want to give the audience a hint of a scene. No more than that. Give them too much and they won't contribute anything themselves. Give them just a suggestion and you get them working with you. That's what gives the theater meaning: when it becomes a social act."

Orson Welles

Your idea may be something specific, like the example above. Or you might simply have a notion of an activity that could help get your coachee's juices flowing, such as proposing a change of scene, taking a break from thinking about the issue and then coming back to it fresh, or brainstorming with some creative colleagues. Whatever occurs and however it happens, if you're confronted with someone who is frustrated and "stuck," and you sense that your idea may help break through that wall, go for it. Put it on the table and see the energy level rise.

Some suggestions to generate energy and action

- ▼ How would you feel about telecommuting one day a week?

- ▼ Do you think an off-site retreat could help diffuse the tensions in the team and help get people back in a positive collaborating mode?

- ▼ You talk a lot about how much you like to collaborate and how much you enjoy the feedback, so I understand your frustration in working solo on this project. How would you feel about taking advantage of the mentoring program here?

- ▼ What about leading the meeting yourself this time?

- ▼ I was thinking that the company fitness program could be a great idea for helping you feel more energetic and motivated. How do you feel about looking into it?

- ▼ Would you want to speak with Tina about this? She was in a similar boat last year.

- ▼ What about some courses at the university?

- ▼ Have you thought about sitting in on those meetings to help you get going in that area?

JUMP-START NEW THINKING

Manager   "So you said you're feeling your team meetings aren't that productive."

Joe   "Yeah. I feel like we're just going through the motions. There's always an agenda to cover. Marge takes notes. We go through the list. Stan talks too much. Susan rarely talks at all. The work gets done, but I sense folks just aren't that engaged. To be honest, it does all feel kind of blah..."

Manager   "How do you develop the agenda?"

Joe   "Well, it sort of develops itself, based on what we decide at the previous week's meeting. I put it together."

Manager   "Have you considered changing things up a bit?"

Joe   "Not really. But now that you mention it, maybe a new format would improve things."

Manager   "What could be different?"

Joe   "Well, you asked about the agenda. Maybe I could ask for suggestions during the week, get everyone's input, and see what surfaces. At least that way everyone will have a chance to weigh in."

Manager   "Great idea. What else could you do?"

Joe   "Hmmm. Maybe I could give everyone a turn at running the meeting..."

All the manager did here was ask a few "suggestive questions." She queried about how the meeting agenda gets developed and wondered if Joe had considered a different approach. In a way, those two suggestive questions triggered new thinking about what the meetings could be. Joe was suddenly thinking of new ways to involve his team in the process of designing the meetings and giving them more responsibility in actually running them. These steps themselves suggest opportunities for more engagement.

Great minds DON'T always think alike...

"If everyone is thinking alike then somebody isn't thinking."

George S. Patton

Some suggestions to jump-start new thinking

▾ Can you see some benefit in shadowing him to learn more about his workday and how you would feel about succeeding him when he moves?

▾ You say you often feel siloed in your work. This update report you sent to the group could really benefit a lot of people across the company. How do you feel about having it posted on the intranet newsletter?

▾ As you say, you've been up against these budgeting deadlines every cycle. How would you feel about moving up the deliverable dates for each department so you could actually be working ahead?

▾ We already have the money budgeted, so how would you feel about bringing in the project management consultant to help you guys get the project rolling?

▾ What if you worked on some sort of monthly bonus or prize for the person who comes up with the most innovative idea?

_____

_____

_____

Enhance an Action Plan

Manager "We're looking at reorganizing some functions around here. We want to have you take on a newly created position that will bridge marketing and product development. It will mean two more people reporting to you and of course more authority with the product team."

Carla "Wow. Thanks for the vote of confidence."

Manager "It's clear you've been developing your leadership skills, and you've done a great job in handling the friction I know you've had to deal with on your team. Really impressive, Carla. You even set clear ground rules for Cynthia, who can be a loose cannon, as we've discussed."

Carla "Your coaching has really helped me. But I'm still having some trouble with thinking on my feet. You *know*, my style is more reflective. I'm much more comfortable stepping back and planning rather than turning on a dime."

Manager "That has its advantages. But I remember when you said if you had voiced your opinion at the time, you might have had more impact. Like the last meeting with the retailers. Didn't you say it took you another whole week to get them on the phone so you could respond to what they proposed—when you had actually been in the same room when they proposed it?"

Carla "Yeah, right. And they took my silence as total agreement when I really saw things differently. I just hadn't decided how to present my case. I do think this will be even more important working with the product development guys. My default mode still seems to be to pull back and take a wait-and-see."

Manager "This could totally not be your thing. But I just had a thought... have you ever considered taking an improv course? That's all about thinking on your feet."

Carla "What a concept! Hmmm.... I might just look into that."

Here, the manager has an in-the-moment insight. Previously, Carla identified her hesitancy to respond on her feet as something holding her back. Her manager has come to recognize this too. Yet even though this theme keeps surfacing, he hadn't considered an improv course before. Curiously, he responds on his feet in offering this creative suggestion.

Some suggestions to enhance an action plan

▾ He says your mentoring has helped him a lot. I know you're serious about doing more public speaking. Have you considered speaking at the regional conference? I'm putting together a panel presentation on our mentoring program.

▾ Of course you can use the interview script as a go-by. I know this is your first time doing this, but you're very personable and insightful. Sure, you can add your questions if they seem appropriate. What do you think about inviting them to ask you questions too?

▾ So, the three of you are jockeying for the corner office at our new digs. You said you don't want this to get contentious, and you've tried to come up with a compelling reason why each of you should have it. But the decision is still not settled. Have you considered just drawing straws?

▾ Thanks for agreeing to stand in at the press conference. I know it can be a challenge if you haven't done this before. Even though Josh has an awful flu and he can't be here, how about giving him a call at home? He might have some pointers for you.

_____

_____

_____

Offer Another Point of View

Buried in the title of this book is a suggestion to consider another point of view: "What could happen if you do nothing?"

Offering another point of view can mean

- ▾ Taking a different perspective or angle into consideration, such as the completely opposite point of view

- ▾ Contemplating something in terms of its own value or importance, rather than giving it equal weight with more pressing matters

- ▾ Figure-ground considerations such as looking at the pros in a discussion and not the cons, or focusing on opportunities instead of obstacles

- ▾ Stepping into someone else's shoes to consider their potential view on the matter, to appreciate that other stakeholders have their own realities, and to gain a fuller understanding

- ▾ Thinking more holistically by stepping outside one's own defined sphere to consider how one's individual actions align with the team, the unit, and the business

- ▾ Gaining perspective by "going to the balcony" to get a bird's-eye view rather than being swept up in the swirl of activity below

_____

_____

_____

Some suggestions to offer another point of view

- ▾ How would you feel about setting up a meeting with Ron and getting his input on this?

- ▾ How might it work to put Amy in charge of the project while you're on vacation rather than compromising your time and trying to work when you really should be away from all this?

- ▾ What impact could it have if you miss the meeting?

- ▾ How does your milestone plan mesh with the sales calendar? The sales guys won't be able to help you with this if they're not available.

- ▾ Do you feel this warrants a focus group? It might really help to know how customers view this.

Both sides now

"The second assault on the same problem should come from a totally different direction."

Tom Hirshfield, American physicist

- If you postpone the meeting until next month, how might that benefit the team?

- Have you considered talking with Meredith about the negotiation workshop she attended this month? It could be something you'd be interested in taking when it's offered again in February.

_____

_____

_____

How to suggest

Alex   "I'm having a hard time with work right now. I know I chose to take this job, but the travel has me a bit frazzled. And now, since the budget was slashed, we all have to work twice as hard."

Manager   "Sounds like you need to vent!"

Alex   "Exactly! But I can't really change anything, can I? Part of me feels like maybe I'm in the wrong job."

Manager   "How is that? Tell me more."

Alex   "Look, I'm willing to roll up my sleeves like everyone else. It's just that this job has changed so much. I never signed up for travel. I really thought I'd have more resources to work with. I just feel like I'm wearing a suit that once fit but doesn't anymore."

Manager   "We'd really hate to lose you. What do you think is frustrating you the most?"

Alex   "Hmmm... The extra workload isn't the biggest piece for me. I can probably deal better with the travel if I turn in earlier the night before hitting the road. I've just been keeping late nights in general. I guess it's really the confidentiality piece that keeps me awake nights. All this secrecy about the new product. Not being able to talk over the particulars of my workday with someone— even my girlfriend. The new confidentiality requirements and pre-launch paranoia have me wound up about everything else."

Manager	"So, being able to talk with someone outside your group would be a help?"
Alex	"Yeah. I know, impossible, right? I've thought about this over and over…"
Manager	"Can I share some information with you?"
Alex	"Sure. Unless it's confidential!"
Manager	"Ha, ha, no worries. Actually, we have a couple of outside coaches. They're top people, and they're under a confidentiality agreement. Chatting with them once a week or so is really working for some of our development people with exactly your dilemma. Is that something that would interest you?"
Alex	"Yes, actually, I'd love to give it a go. When can I start?"

Even in everyday conversations with friends or family, making a suggestion can be greeted with enthusiasm, or fraught with ill feeling. In business, you will be trying primarily to meet the needs and goals of the business through meeting those of your people. In this environment, where expertise, ego, reputation, and competing hierarchies may be at stake, it can be a minefield. Knowing how to introduce a suggestion effectively will increase your chances of improving performance.

Once you have mastered the "when" of suggesting, the "how" can be handled in a variety of ways.

With Permission

When a coachee is stuck, you can ask permission to offer some input. A simple, friendly "Could I make a suggestion?" is usually enough to both demonstrate respect for, and pique the interest of, your coachee. Asking permission is especially useful when a conversation is delicate or the stakes are high.

Ways to request permission

- ▾ Is this a good time?

- ▾ Would it be OK with you to spend more time thinking about…?

- ▾ I'd like to go a little deeper into this. How does that sound?

- ▾ I get a sense you have more to say about that. Can I probe a little further?

- ▾ Could I ask you a few more specific questions around that?

- ▾ Can we spend a few minutes testing some ideas around this?

- ▾ Can I offer a few ideas about how to prioritize your work?

- ▾ Can I stretch you a little on this?

- ▾ Can I challenge you a little on this?

- ▾ Would you be interested in trying a different way to view it if you get a different result?

WITH APPROPRIATE FRAMING

In the dialogue above about dealing with intense confidentiality, the suggestion is framed in a way that is palatable to the coachee. It is offered almost casually, acknowledging that other people with the very same problem are benefiting from it. Framing issues in the context of the coach's experience can normalize the situation and can make the suggestion seem much less threatening or risky. Having a "shared" experience raises the comfort level and increases trust.

Ways to use appropriate framing

- ▾ The research has shown…

- ▾ The data demonstrate…

- ▾ We've sometimes found that…

- ▾ A new spin might produce some new answers. What do you think about…?

- ▾ Sometimes it's worth throwing caution to the wind. How would you feel about taking a chance on this one?

- ▾ We each have our own style of learning. Have you considered whether she's more a visual learner? What could you do to accommodate that?

With Acknowledgment

A suggestion will likely follow a series of ideas from the coachee. An acknowledgment of the merit of his ideas and the professional value of the coachee is key to getting a useful suggestion across.

Ways to use acknowledgment

- ▾ I know you want to be involved. Your writing is so strong—how would you feel about drafting the new proposal?

- ▾ Your troubleshooting here has helped us get over some hurdles. The Detroit office could really use your help…

maybe for a few months. This might fit with your wanting a change. How would this sit with you?

▾ You said you like the detail, and you're so good at it. Would you consider coordinating the September meeting?

▾ You're asking great questions. How would you feel about doing an informational interview with him?

▾ You know so much about the history of this project. Would you be interested in helping mar-com write a piece about it in the newsletter?

WITH PERSPECTIVE

As we have discussed, being aware of differing perspectives is essential. Looking at the context, you can choose your words and your approach with an awareness of both the big picture and the coachee's individual viewpoint. For example, he may be thrilled to hear your idea; alternatively it may not play well with his sense of pride. He may be a real team player in personality, happy with input from anyone, or more used to working solo. In offering her own perspective, the manager/coach often has to be willing to give a bit of herself—to share a personal experience—in getting the other person to open up.

Ways to use perspective

▾ Something that worked for me was…

▾ I've read a bit about this and am wondering if you've ever considered…

- ▾ I just had an idea, if you'd like to hear it.

- ▾ What you're saying just made me think of something you might want to check out.

- ▾ Do you want a suggestion from me?

- ▾ Would you like some input on that?

- ▾ I think I have something that might be useful here.

- ▾ I just thought of something you could add to that list if you're interested.

- ▾ There's a great website I've used for what you're thinking about.

_____

_____

_____

It's important to respect the coachee's intelligence and expertise. So, offer suggestions in a manner the coachee won't consider patronizing. Diplomacy and sensitivity offer your best entrée into the new territory opened by a suggestion. You needn't walk on eggshells! Just be sure your suggestions are nonthreatening, nonjudgmental, and nonprescriptive. Your suggestion shouldn't be a demand in disguise—though you hope it will move both your coachee and the company forward. Put your own expectations aside. She may not agree with you. Still, you have planted a seed, so there's always the chance it may take!

Tuneful advice

"Just a spoonful of sugar helps the medicine go down..."

Mary Poppins

What to suggest

Suggestions, like ideas, are a dime a dozen, but there could be a gem among those dozens. So, if you've got the "when" and "how" down, serve it up. It's the coachee's decision whether to follow up on your idea or to simply consider the different perspective you've introduced.

Suggestions can be clustered in infinite ways. Here are some different kinds of suggestions:

- ▼ Experiential learning:
  classes, travel, interactions, informational interviews, shadowing

- ▼ Networking and reaching out to others:
  professional associations, conferences, meet-ups, industry events, online social or professional networks

- ▼ Point-of-view considerations:
  stakeholder perspectives, outside consultants, mentors

- ▼ Learning resources:
  books, websites, articles, podcasts, webinars, professional association offerings

- ▼ Out-of-comfort-zone experiences:
  difficult conversations, new responsibilities, new roles, new behaviors

_____

_____

_____

- ▼ You're asking great questions for someone who's only been on board here for a month. I was wondering how you would feel about shadowing one of our sales folks for a day. It could offer you a fuller picture of how what we do here in marketing helps salespeople do their jobs. Pam would be happy to have you go along with her on some calls.

- ▼ Are you aware that the company covers tuition for most classes for professional development?

- ▼ Do you think a factory tour could help answer some of your questions?

- ▼ Have you ever sought informational interviews?

- ▼ How would you feel about working together with corporate communications on that?

_____

_____

_____

Networking and Reaching Out to Others

- ▼ Are you familiar with the BDI Group on LinkedIn? It's international. Basically, it's a platform for marketing, communications, and media professionals to network. It could prove helpful to bounce some of this stuff off some of your peers out there.

- ▼ Did you know that Toastmasters has a regional group here? Their monthly meetings encourage members to present. Could be another opportunity to develop those speaking skills.

▼ Innovation is the theme of their upcoming conference. I have the schedule of workshops and presenters. Would you like to take a look?

_____

_____

_____

POINT-OF-VIEW CONSIDERATIONS

▼ You acknowledged that you guys don't usually collaborate upstream in these situations. What might you gain if the three of you got together to brainstorm some ideas beforehand?

▼ Gee, your team has been wrestling with this project from the get-go. How would you feel about bringing in a PM consultant for an on-site workshop? I know someone we've contracted with in the past who really helped the operations group.

▼ How would you feel about planning a one-day retreat to bring your two groups together? It would be an opportunity to share and exchange ideas and provide everyone with a bigger picture of how the project is proceeding.

_____

_____

_____

Learning Resources

▼ Here's the article I mentioned from last month's *HBR*.

▼ You might want to look into the webinar that AMA is offering on the topic next month.

▼ You mentioned you read his other book too. It was reviewed on 800 CEO Read. Are you familiar with that site?

_____

_____

_____

Out-of-Comfort-Zone Experiences

▼ She's taking a six-month leave of absence. How would you feel about stepping in as acting project manager?

▼ You're really clear about the benefits of doing this. I know you're more comfortable sharing your take with me or just sending an email to Jasper. But what about asking him to schedule you for ten minutes on the agenda to present your case to the group?

▼ I understand she can be a bear when defending her turf. You say she really responds to data—have you considered having this conversation after sending her your analysis?

▼ You had said you wanted to work on your confidence in presenting in front of larger audiences. So how was it representing your group at the regional meeting?

_____

_____

_____

Suggesting: What's the big idea?

Accepting your suggestion involves a certain amount of risk for the coachee: dipping the proverbial toe into the water. Acknowledge that. If appropriate, talk about trial and error, the importance of failing occasionally, the unlikelihood of experiencing success without taking risk. Even if he doesn't follow your suggestion, simply exploring it can trigger insights and self-awareness that will help your coachee take some other—possibly related—action to meet his objectives. Remember to offer suggestions rather than give advice. That way, if your coachee chooses to act on your suggestion, he owns it!

| "What could happen if you do nothing?"

4. Conversation Maps

As we've seen, conversations grow organically. There's nothing neat and tidy about them. Listening, asking, and suggesting are not discrete activities. They are integrated parts of a dialogue that feed off one another. This section presents a few maps of conversations that demonstrate how such dialogues evolve and how, at various junctures, they can travel in very different directions.

As the exchanges progress, the content suggests different paths to follow, each offering potentially different outcomes. Some simply suggest different routes that arrive at the same outcome. Again, this doesn't mean that a coaching conversation follows a conscious strategy. Rather, the maps suggest how the whole is the sum of its parts. Most important, they should bring home the significance of considering the person with whom you're talking (his or her style of communication) and of being in the moment and letting the conversation lead *you*, rather than you lead the conversation.

Situation 1: Managing up

Laura is Ted's senior manager. She has assigned Ted and his team an unreasonable amount of work to do. Ted wants to do a good job and deliver results, but feels he can't because of the workload and its impact on his team.

Coaching Skills and Competencies

Acknowledgment, sensitivity to other's learning and communication style, guiding collaborative process in meeting a challenge, open-ended questioning.

Laura Hi, Ted. Come on in.

Conversation A

Ted We really need to talk about things.

Laura Sounds serious.

Ted Not serious. Just that my guys are really overloaded.

Laura How's that?

Ted Malcolm has been out sick and Audrey and David have had to pick up his load. George is working with the new hire on the budget items at the same time he's helping train her on the system.

Laura What *is* getting done? What are you asking for here?

Conversation B

Ted Thanks for squeezing me in today.

Laura Sure. What's up?

Ted There's an awful lot on our plate right now, and I honestly don't feel the team can meet all these expectations. They're working overtime as it is. I'm hoping you might help us get through this crunch without setting everyone's hair on fire.

Laura What's your thinking on this?

Ted Everything has been given top priority, which doesn't make sense. Here's an overview of all our projects and the major milestones. I thought we could analyze things and focus on what's most important. Can you help us find a place to loosen the schedule up a bit?

Laura Seeing all the projects lined up like this is helpful. I understand your problem. How about we delay the Carlyle packaging deadlines two weeks? Also, I can talk with Ralph about sharing some of the prep of the sales materials.

Analysis

These two conversations map entirely differently from the start, given Ted's different approaches to the same challenge.

In Conversation A, Ted opens the dialogue with a do matic, urgent tone. Then he seems to retreat defensively. He introduces the situation with an explanation of the problem rather than offering a solution. All in all, he hasn't considered how to talk to Laura so she will understand his concerns and help him generate a solution. As a consequence, Laura isn't very forthcoming or collaborative and responds by putting him on the defensive.

Conversation B presents a totally different approach. Here, Ted acknowledges Laura's time constraints and expresses his appreciation for Laura's making herself available. Basically, Ted has set the stage for a more open and friendly exchange. He explains the reality of the situation, its impact on his people, and his desire to take some action to improve things. Laura responds by inviting his input to reach a solution. Ted has come prepared with his overview and proposes a diagnostic approach to reach a solution. This should appeal to Laura, whom Ted knows prefers clear reasoning and analysis. This enables Laura to fully understand the challenge and to collaborate in generating some solutions.

Situation 2: A Change Effort

Phil is Maxine's manager. He wants to impress on her the impact of recent declines in revenue and the budgetary changes that have become a necessary response. As a senior manager, he recognizes the importance of communicating early and often and wants to include Maxine in the decision process.

Coaching Skills and Competencies

Listening actively, acknowledging, digging deeper to expand thinking, asking open-ended questions that offer the coachee opportunities to create her own solutions to meet the challenge of cutbacks and its impact on her group.

Phil I'm getting back to you to talk about the changes coming down. I want you in the loop so I can get your input and so you can keep your team informed.

Conversation A

Maxine Geez, I hope we're not losing positions. We're overwhelmed as it is.

→ **1**

Phil Why do you think you'll be losing positions?

↓

Maxine I figure jobs are the first cuts to consider.

Phil We may have to make some cuts.

→ **2**

↓

Maxine Are you cutting positions, or are other kinds of scaling back being considered?

Conversation B

Maxine I appreciate your keeping me on top of things.

→ **1**

Phil I understand Jenny is moving away. We probably won't be filling that position. What can your group do to adjust to one fewer person on the team?

Phil Forecasts for the first quarter have been scaled back considerably. We are looking at reducing costs 10-15% across all departments. How might you consider handling this with the least impact?

→ **2**

Phil We're considering a host of cost-reduction opportunities. How would you feel about putting together a brief proposal with forecasts for savings you can make from *your* budget?

Maxine Sure. How about we reconnect on this on Friday?

Phil I look forward to your analysis and ideas.

Maxine Wow! We've just begun interviewing to fill Jenny's spot. I guess we need to put the brakes on that. Is there any other way we could cut cost? I bet we'll wind up having to outsource some of the design work. Jenny is a workhorse, and everyone else is wall-to-wall with deadlines.

Phil I apologize for any time you've invested in interviewing. Outsourcing remains a possibility, although I think I hear some antipathy to that? What do you suggest as an alternative?

Maxine I *am* ambivalent about outsourcing. I like developing and working with my own people. How about I see where else we could cut costs?

Phil That would be great. What else could you do?

Maxine I'll do a cost analysis of what outsourcing some of the work would mean. May as well see if there are some cost benefits to that option.

Phil Terrific! Let's meet again Friday. Will that give you enough time?

Maxine I need to put some think on it. I'll take a look at my budget for possible ways to trim. When will you know for sure?

Phil Let's meet again Friday. I may have a better idea about the numbers, and you'll have more time to think about how you might reconfigure your budget.

Analysis

The outcomes of all the dialogue threads above are similar. Maxine will work with her budget to consider how to allocate her cutbacks. However, in the middle conversation Phil listens well and picks up on Maxine's ambivalence regarding outsourcing, and he opens the way for her to explain. Further, Phil encourages her to expand her thinking. This results in her offering to do a cost analysis of freelance hiring. Maxine takes ownership of the action rather than waiting for Phil to make the request of her. In the third thread (B2), Phil asks an open-ended question that invites Maxine's input. In response, it is Maxine herself who comes up with the idea to analyze her budget to look for savings options.

Situation 3: Recruitment Standards

Jasper is technology director, and Mary is operations manager for a small software company. Jasper is seeking Mary's advice. He is frustrated with the candidates for an open technology position because they seem unimaginative and indifferent. He wants to maintain his high technical standards but also wants people with passion and energy.

Coaching Skills and Competencies

Listening intently; digging deeper to encourage the coachee to consider options, alternatives, and more innovative solutions to his challenge; paraphrasing; clarifying; acknowledging.

Mary Come in. You said you wanted to talk about the candidates for the IT position.

Conversation A

Jasper Where to start...I've been interviewing people for the past week or so, trying to find the right person to fill this seat.

Mary But I'm hearing some dissatisfaction. What's going on?

Jasper The candidates I'm getting seem to be looking more for a job than an opportunity. They have big-company tech experience, which is good, but they're missing something.

Mary How can you tell the difference?

Jasper They're so focused on the package and don't seem curious about the business or opportunities for advancement. I'm desperate to fill this position, however...

Conversation B

Jasper The candidates for the IT position are like walking stiffs.

1

Mary Walking stiffs?

Jasper They offer up a lot of yes/no answers, but getting any information out of them is like pulling teeth. The enthusiasm meter is low.

Jasper Not to stereotype, but you IT guys seem to attract the more introverted and nonverbal among us.

2

Mary That can be true. But look at Art or Jennifer—life of the party and everyone who worked with them said they were dependable and on-target problem solvers. I can't imagine these new candidates winning hearts and minds.

Mary You seem to be saying it's just as important to find someone who's a cultural fit and not give in to the pressure of having a tech-competent person who won't make it in the company. I would agree. But the candidates so far don't seem to fill the bill. Am I right?

Jasper Yeah, do we want to bring in a clock puncher?

Mary What sort of questions did you ask to get this lack of initiative that's frustrating you?

Jasper Well, I ask where they see themselves in three years. But they seem to describe where they are now (or would be if we hire them).

Mary That's always a good question. What else have you asked?

Jasper Hmmm. I ask if they have any questions about the business. But the people I've talked with just say "No, not really." One guy just wanted to know about the dress code.

Mary Anything else you asked?

Jasper Geez, they didn't pick up on these two invitatoins to jump into the future and learn more about us and where we're going. I sorta was stopped in my tracks.

Mary Where else could you go with them?

Jasper I suppose I could ask what excites them professionally. Maybe that could trigger some thinking about what matters.

Jasper I suppose I could sharpen up the requirements statement. Maybe I focused too much on technical chops and not enough on small company culture.

Mary That might provide some context for questioning. What else could you do?

Jasper I could bring in Bart Stevens to join me. He's an engineer; basically a techie himself. Maybe having a colleague in the mix will help tease out more information from the from these prospects.

Mary That sounds like a good idea. It would offer another perspective. Anything else you could do?

Jasper I think I'll pursue those options for now and see where that gets us. Could just be this batch of candidates. But I may as well explore these other options. Thanks for talking me through this one.

Jasper Yeah. I'm going to hold out for another week or so and keep on interviewing. I just know these choices won't sit well with folks here.

Mary That might turn up some more appropriate candidates, but it will take more time. What can you do in the interviews you have coming up?

Analysis

Asking the same question differently can encourage a coachee to dig deeper for alternative solutions. Mary gently prods Jasper to look at options he hadn't considered before. The conversation map demonstrates the various paths their dialogue can take.

Mary continues pushing Jasper to mine for unexplored opportunities. Her prompting also gets him to recognize the social value of past IT people, and to include a technically savvy colleague early in his interviewing process.

Situation 4: Gaps in performance

Chloe, director of marketing, wants to be sure Ed, a sales veteran, is prepared to move forward with the new integrated marketing strategy.

Coaching Skills and Competencies

Careful listening for what is *not* said, reading between the lines, following themes, digging deeper, knowing how and when to make a suggestion to help facilitate finding a solution

Chloe I set up this time to talk to you because at the sales meeting I sensed you're not totally on board with the new integrated marketing strategy. You seemed distracted.

Conversation A

Ed I had no idea I was sending that messge.

Chloe So everything is good with you?

Ed Yeah. I'm fine with the plan.

Chloe So you feel you can meet the sales goals?

Ed Well, the projections look pretty rosy, to be honest.

Chloe Do you think they're too optimistic? I'm hearing some skepticism.

Conversation B

Ed You sure read me right.

1

Chloe So what's at issue?

Ed I think I'm not clear on what I'm not clear on.

Chloe Well you're clear enough about your lack of clarity. Maybe we should start with what you know.

2

Chloe Can you explain what's not working for you?

Ed I'm just trying to get with the multiplatform balancing act.

Chloe OK. What seems to be the problem?

Ed Maybe you're reading me better than I'm at reading myself. I'm still a little green with all the online options and how attractive the bundling with digital, print and radio will work for my accounts. Everything is intergrated these days and it makes sense, but the pricing and positioning are new for me.

Ed I know print. I know TV. I am slowly getting up to speed on digital.

Chloe You're an ace in print and TV. But I wonder if adding all of this means we shouldn't give you support.

Ed It really is the mix and match and, yes, the pricing options, and how the various programs best meet the needs of my accounts. I think it is that I need to be more familiar with all the positioning arguments before I can turn around and make them.

Ed It's a little on the pricing. But when I really think about it, it's more than that.

Chloe How so?

Ed Maybe its just that I'm not yet comfortable pitching these more integrated approaches. I especially need to work on making the case for shifting more dollars to the digital options, away from print. You know I come from print, so it feels like I'm stealing from myself. But marketing surely has some powerful research to support all this.

Chloe How would you feel if you had someone from marketing with you when you do your presentations? I'm sure we can schedule Janice or Rob to accompany you on some calls to add a little marketing muscle.

Ed That would be really great. Makes a lot of sense.

Analysis

Chloe listens beyond what is said and is able to read body language. These skills enable her to pick up on Ed's ambivalence—a real departure from his usual focus and energy. Both in the open forum of the sales meeting and in her one-on-one with Ed, Chloe identifies Ed's roadblock to accepting the integrated media sales strategy. She reaches beyond Ed's stated words and encourages him to take a broader look at what bothers him about the new plan. Once he recognizes the real issue, she steps in with an appropriate suggestion that he welcomes and wants to pursue.

| "What could happen if you do nothing?"

What's the big idea?

You may have read straight through this handbook. Or you may have skimmed or browsed here and there. Either way, keep it handy. Flag useful pages, earmark, highlight, and add your own questions—building on the lists begun here. Use it! Work those listening, asking, and suggesting muscles. You will develop coaching skills that will serve you well in managing your people, and yourself. Above all, you will be developing the talent of your talent (your people). They, and the business itself, will be the beneficiaries of your coaching conversations.

Acknowledgements

Heartfelt thanks to Alice Larsen of New Day Company, Anders Fleischer of RighThought, and Janice Taylor of Janice Taylor Living for their thoughtfulness in reviewing the manuscript and offering such constructive advice. Their input has helped make this handbook more relevant to the real day-to-day challenges that managers encounter at work. Their professional insights will help generate better, more collaborative coaching conversations and a more open style of leading people to reach their potential.

Authors

Jane Murphy is a partner in Giraffe Business Publishing LLC and Giraffe LLC, a consulting firm that designs custom solutions to help organizations improve the management capabilities of their people. Jane also leads Giraffe's coaching engagements, working with clients to solve business and leadership challenges. Jane has been principal and co-founder of several publishing ventures, including KIDVIDZ, which won numerous awards for its special-interest videos. She has received grants from the National Endowment for the Humanities and the Rockefeller Foundation and served as an advisor to Tufts University and Grolier Publishing. In addition to a master's in education, Jane has professional certification in executive and organizational coaching from New York University. She also has a professional certificate from New York's Institute of Culinary Education and a diploma from the London Film School. She is a member of the International Coaching Federation and the Women's National Book Association. She has co-authored several books, including STAY TUNED! (Doubleday) and The Great Big Burger Book (Harvard Common Press). She speaks regularly on custom and special-market publishing.

Khatun Huber is a facilitator, writer, and executive coach working with professionals in advertising, finance, and the scientific communities. A member of the International Coaching Federation, she is certified by New York University in executive coaching and organizational development. She is also trained by Wilderness Medical Associates as a search-and-rescue professional specializing in remote environments and urban mass-casualty disaster scenarios. A volunteer for the Red Cross Disaster Reserve, Huber also sits on the advisory board of Amend.org, a nonprofit addressing childhood road traffic injury in Africa. She has also been a regular commentator on Sirius (FM) radio on coaching and other subjects.